Presented by

THE BIRCH FAMILY AND FRIENDS

IN MEMORY OF

WILLIAM "BILL" BIRCH

2004

MODERN WORLD NATIONS

AFGHANISTAN	IRAQ
ARGENTINA	IRELAND
AUSTRALIA	ISRAEL
AUSTRIA	ITALY
BAHRAIN	JAMAICA
BERMUDA	JAPAN
BOLIVIA	KAZAKHSTAN
BOSNIA AND HERZEGOVINA	KENYA
BRAZIL	KUWAIT
CANADA	MEXICO
CHILE	THE NETHERLANDS
CHINA	NEW ZEALAND
COSTA RICA	NIGERIA
CROATIA	NORTH KOREA
CUBA	NORWAY
EGYPT	PAKISTAN
ENGLAND	PERU
ETHIOPIA	RUSSIA
FRANCE	SAUDI ARABIA
REPUBLIC OF GEORGIA	SCOTLAND
GERMANY	SOUTH AFRICA
GHANA	SOUTH KOREA
GUATEMALA	TAIWAN
ICELAND	TURKEY
INDIA	UKRAINE
IRAN	UZBEKISTAN

Chile

Richard A. Crooker
Kutztown University

Series Consulting Editor
Charles F. Gritzner
South Dakota State University

CHELSEA HOUSE
PUBLISHERS
A Haights Cross Communications Company

Philadelphia

Frontispiece: Flag of Chile

Cover: Reflections of the Andes Mountains

CHELSEA HOUSE PUBLISHERS

VP, New Product Development Sally Cheney
Director of Production Kim Shinners
Creative Manager Takeshi Takahashi
Manufacturing Manager Diann Grasse

Staff for CHILE

Executive Editor Lee Marcott
Production Editor Megan Emery
Picture Research 21st Century Publishing and Communications, Inc.
Series Designer Takeshi Takahashi
Cover Designer Keith Trego
Layout 21st Century Publishing and Communications, Inc.

A Haights Cross Communications ◀━ Company

JNF
983
Crooke

http://www.chelseahouse.com

First Printing

1 3 5 7 9 8 6 4 2

Library of Congress Cataloging-in-Publication Data

Crooker, Richard A.
   Chile/by Richard A. Crooker.
      v. cm.—(Modern world nations)
Includes bibliographical references and index.
Contents: Physical landscapes—Chile through time—People and culture—Government
and politics—Economy—Living in Chile today—Chile looks ahead.
   ISBN 0-7910-7912-0
   1. Chile—Juvenile literature. [1. Chile.] I. Title. II. Series.
F3058.5.C76 2004
983—dc22

2003028098

Table of Contents

Chile

CHAPTER

1

Introduction

C hile has a little of everything. It is rich in copper, fruits, forests, and fish. It is a country of dramatic scenery and many climates. Cool waters stroke its shore and icy glaciers crown its peaks. Sighs of volcanoes and jolts of earthquakes shake its ribs. Squeezed between the heights of the mountains and the depths of the sea, Chile is a geologic marvel. Despite this physical diversity, a sense of nationhood among its people unifies the country.

Chile is situated on the extreme southwestern coast of South America. The Pacific Ocean lies to the west; Argentina and Bolivia are to the east. No country in the world has such an extraordinary shape as Chile. Its territory consists of a long, narrow ribbon of land that runs north to south for approximately 2,700 miles (4,400 kilometers). Its maximum width is barely 100 miles (160 kilometers). With an area of 292,260 square miles (756,950 square kilometers), Chile is a little smaller than Texas. The nation has the world's driest desert and

Chile is located on the southwestern coast of South America, with the Pacific Ocean to the west and Argentina and Bolivia to the east. The country has a very unusual shape, consisting of a narrow strip of land running approximately 2,700 miles (4,345 km) along the South American coast. However, its maximum width is less than 100 miles (161 km) and its total area of 292,260 square miles (756,950 square kilometers) makes it slightly smaller than Texas.

some of the highest mountains. Approximately 70 percent of the land is mountainous, as the Andes Mountains extend the length of the country and form a natural barrier between Argentina and Bolivia.

Chile's name has no connection with the Spanish word "chili," as in chili pepper, but the words are pronounced the same. Most scholars believe that the name Chile comes from a native Indian word—*Tchilli*, meaning "snow" or "cold." The Indians lived in a valley not far from where the country's capital and largest city, Santiago, is today. They named the valley *Tchilli* because cold air and snow would blow into the lowland from Andean peaks. The similarity in the meaning of the native word *Tchilli* to the English word "chilly" is simply a coincidence.

This odd-shaped country with a strange name is one of the world's most respected nations. Its history of political stability is unmatched in Latin America. Its economic genius helped ignite the global economy of the 1990s. It continues to have one of the fastest growing economies in South America. It is also an honest country, which for a developing nation is unusual. Taxes are actually collected, the police generally do not seek or take bribes, and most politicians are honest.

Chile's location south of the equator means that its seasons are the opposite of those of places like the United States and Europe. Summer officially begins on December 21 and ends on March 21. Winter begins on June 21 and continues until September 21. The reversal in the timing of the summer and winter seasons may not seem important at first. In some respects, however, life in Chile is upside down compared to ours. Chileans celebrate Christmas just like we do, only in the hottest time of the year. Imagine decorating a Christmas tree with tinsel and icicles in the heat of summer! On Christmas Day, Chileans can enjoy picnics at the beach or meals in the backyard. Pity the poor fathers who have to dress up in weighty Santa Claus costumes in the summertime, though.

Practically speaking, the opposite seasons help Chile's economy. In January, supermarkets in North America and Europe are selling fruit plucked fresh a few weeks earlier in Chile's Central Valley and Andean foothills. In addition, skiers in the United States and Europe come to Chile's Andean ski resorts from June to the middle of October to extend their ski season.

Other nations envy Chile's physical beauty, democratic tradition, economic success, and attractive culture. Described here is how geography and history converged to create the nation of Chile, as well as an outline of its future problems and prospects. This study begins by examining Chile's diverse physical landscapes, because the land is the stage on which a nation plays out its unique existence.

2

Physical Landscapes

Three major landform regions divide Chile: the Andes Mountains, the coast and islands, and the Central Valley. The regions run north to south and parallel to each other. The Andes region is an awesome mountain barrier. Its majestic peaks of spectacular height and bone-chilling temperatures define the country's eastern border. The nation's coast includes imposing sea cliffs, beautiful beaches, low mountains, ice-scoured valleys, and sparsely settled islands. Squeezed between the Andes and the coast is a long Central Valley. Although Chile is a narrow country, its broad stretch of latitude embraces a variety of climates, ranging from a parched north, a temperate middle, and an extremely wet south. Spread over this crazy-quilt geography is a variety of soils, plants, and animals.

THE ANDES

The high mountain range of the Andes (*Cordillera de Los Andes*

Chile's unique shape results in a great variety of physical features in the country. It boasts beaches, mountains, and ice fields, as well as multiple distinct climates and diverse plant and animal species.

in Spanish) extends like a backbone through the entire length of Chile, separating it from Argentina and Bolivia. Chile's northern Andes are an extension of the Bolivian *altiplano* (Spanish for "high plain"). The altiplano is between 11,000 and 13,000 feet (3,350 to 4,000 meters) in elevation. Cold winds are incessant, and they howl as they blow across the almost featureless plain. The evenness of the general surface is dramatic. Isaiah Bowman was the first U.S. geographer to explore the region. Writing in the early 1900s, he reported that the high plain looked "as if it were cut by a knife drawn along the edge of a ruler." Bowman aptly noted that the surface is not entirely flat. A scattering of cone-shaped volcanoes, lava flows, and mountain ridges rise above the altiplano's generally level surface, reaching 17,000 feet (5,600 meters) in some places.

Farther south is Chile's central Andes region. This area has some of the highest peaks in the world. Mount Aconcagua, the highest summit (22,832 feet or 6,959 meters) in the Western Hemisphere is just across the border in Argentina. Several other prominent peaks are nearby. Together, these summits form one of the most spectacular landscapes in Andean South America. Yet, like forbidden fruit, the inviting summits have dangers, such as landslides, avalanches, earthquakes, and volcanic eruptions. Moreover, the heights endanger aircraft. Before the arrival of passenger jets in the 1960s, pilots, unable to fly above the mountains, had to wait for good weather and find a route between peaks.

The peril of Andean aviation was made famous when, in 1972, a vintage propeller-driven plane carrying rugby players from Uruguay crashed while attempting to fly across the Andes to Santiago, Chile. Some of those aboard died, but others survived the crash and for more than two months struggled against bitter-cold temperatures before being rescued. A book and a film titled *Alive!* immortalize this tragic story.

South of the central Andes, summits average about 6,500 feet (2,000 meters), much lower than the northern and central Andes.

The Andes Mountains extend through the entire length of Chile and separate the country from its neighbors Argentina and Bolivia. The mountain range has some of the highest peaks in the world as well as many active volcanoes.

Geographers call the southern mountains the Patagonian Andes, because the mountains are not much higher than Argentina's adjoining Patagonia Plateau. Summits are low in part because of glacial erosion. During the Ice Age, erosion was widespread. Ice fields (*Campos de Hielos* in Spanish) covered some mountain ridges completely. The ice slowly whittled down summits by plucking and scraping away rock. Today, only two ice fields exist, but they account for nearly 60 percent of the region's total ice surface. Outlet glaciers from the ice fields and smaller valley glaciers grow down the mountains to the ocean's edge, where they calve (break off) to form small icebergs.

The Andes Mountains are youthful because they are still growing. Collisions of sections of Earth's lithosphere (outer rock layer) are causing the mountains to build up. (Geologists call these "colliding sections plates.") The collision involves a large, westward-moving South American plate and three plates that are moving eastward. Gravity is pulling the smaller, heavier plates beneath the South American plate, where they melt to form magma (molten rock). The collision is also causing the western edge of South America to compress, uplift, and fold to create the Andes Mountains. The magma beneath the continent rises to the surface during explosive volcanic eruptions.

Chile ranks fifth among nations in the number of active volcanoes. (Geologists define active volcanoes as those that have erupted within recent centuries.) Chile has 36 active volcanoes; it is behind Russia (52) and ahead of Iceland (18). The country's main volcanoes are south of the latitude of Santiago and include Cerro Azul, Llaima, Villarrica, and Cerro Hudson. Villarrica, which is east of Puerto Montt in southern Chile, is the most active volcano in South America. It has been erupting fitfully since the early 1980s. This peak is also Chile's deadliest volcano. Eruptions in 1949, 1963, 1964, and 1971 caused mudflows that killed 75 people. Fortunately, this is a relatively small number of deaths compared with those caused by volcanoes in other regions of the world.

Chile's landscape also experiences severe earthquakes caused by the strains of plate collision. Indeed, the coastal cities of Valparaíso, Concepción, Valdivia, and Puerto Montt have been leveled or severely shaken by earthquakes in the past 100 years. One of the strongest temblors (earthquakes) of the twentieth century struck in Chile on May 22, 1960. The earthquake created a deadly tsunami (a superstrong ocean wave) that traveled across the Pacific Ocean to Asia in just 24 hours. The earthquake and tsunami killed more than 2,000 people in Chile, Hawaii, Japan, and the Philippines. Because of the unrelenting pressure from colliding plates, Chile will continue to experience severe quakes.

Human use of the Chilean Andes varies among its sub-regions, depending on available resources. In the northern altiplano region, the land is used in the summer to graze livestock. In the winter, tourists take jeep excursions there. The principle economic value of the northern Andes is its water supply for towns in the region. Chile's central and southern Andes offer outdoor enthusiasts many pastimes. Alpine scenery, trout-filled lakes and streams, and snow-covered slopes attract thousands of visitors each year. They come to camp, fish, hike, climb, and ride horses and mountain bikes. Whitewater rafting, water skiing, snow skiing, snow-boarding, and paragliding are also popular. Chileans also depend on the Andes' natural resources. Melted water from snow and ice feeds turbulent rivers. Hydroelectric dams on several of these rivers not only provide electricity, but also supply water to the nation's farmers, homes, and industries. Logging companies harvest the forests for their timber.

COAST AND ISLANDS

Chile and the other Andean countries have an emergent coastline. As the western edge of South America rises out of the sea, erosion and deposition by waves create narrow coastal plains, sea cliffs, headlands, small beaches, and marine terraces. The coastal plains are usually narrow, averaging less than 1 mile

(1.6 kilometers) wide. Where there is no plain, ocean and land engage in a spirited battle. The unrelenting waves inevitably cut wall-like sea cliffs into the land. Areas that are more resistant to wave erosion become cliff-edged headlands (sections of land that jut into the sea). Waves focus most of their rage on the headlands. Between the promontories (land projecting into a body of water), relatively calm waters deposit narrow, curving strips of sandy beaches.

Over time, the relentless waves cut into the land to create wave-planed submarine benches (flat areas). The benches become a stair-step series of marine terraces (*terrazas fluviomarinas*) above the water's edge, as plate convergence gradually forces them out of the sea. Some of these terraces, such as Antofagasta and Tocopilla in northern Chile, are large enough for coastal settlements. There are only a few good deepwater harbors. They are all situated in valley openings that have protection from storms.

Chile's southern coastline begins south of Puerto Montt. During the Ice Age, glaciers grew out of the southern Andes. Westward-moving tongues of ice gouged huge depressions in the Central Valley and coast range. After the Ice Age ended, about 10,000 years ago, glaciers worldwide melted. The glacial melt water poured into ocean basins to raise sea level to its present height. Along Chile's southern coast range, areas that were not eroded by the ice became a forest-covered chain of islands (archipelago). Ocean water filled the ice-scoured Central Valley, and narrow arms of the sea (fjords) flooded into the glaciated valleys of the Andes. The rugged, broken shoreline of Chile's south bears a strong similarity to other glaciated mountainous coastlines, such as those of Norway and western Canada.

Chile's coast range (*cordillera de la Costa*) rises abruptly from the shoreline. The range consists of a narrow, level-topped plateau. Elevations are greatest in the central area that separates Santiago from Valparaíso, but heights never exceed

6,500 feet (2,000 meters). The north to south trending range gradually decreases in elevation from the central area to less than 3,280 feet (1,000 meters) at both ends. The northern end is at the Peru border. The southern end is the Zarao Mountains, a north south spine of upland that runs down the middle of Chiloé Island.

The country has many islands. Beginning at Chiloé, most of them are strung out along the country's glacially scoured southern coast. Chile shares with Argentina the island of *Tierra del Fuego*, which sits at the very southern end of South America. The island's name means "Land of Fire" in Spanish. Chile also owns a number of oceanic islands. The San Félix and San Ambrosio islands are roughly 465 miles (750 kilometers) west of Chile. The Juan Fernández islands are about the same distance away but farther south. The latter are known for the fact that one of them was the home for five years (1704 to 1709) of Alexander Selkirk. Selkirk was a foul-tempered, quarrelsome sailor; the captain of Selkirk's ship became fed up with him and marooned him on one of the islands. Selkirk's real-life experience became the basis for the novel *Robinson Crusoe,* written by Daniel Defoe wrote in 1719. The classic story, which Defoe placed in the Caribbean Sea, became so famous that the Chilean government renamed Selkirk's island Robinson Crusoe Island in the mid-1970s.

Easter Island is also part of Chile. This solitary island is famous for its monumental statues carved from the island's volcanic rocks. The origin of these statues is a mystery. This tiny speck of land is 2,350 miles (3,780 kilometers) off the Chilean coast. Because of its interesting monuments, Easter Island has become an important stopover on South Pacific airline routes.

THE CENTRAL VALLEY

The Central Valley is a series of long, narrow basins of

Chile's long coastline and many islands are some of its most notable characteristics. The country's most famous island is Easter Island, seen above, known for its mysterious statues of unknown origins carved from volcanic rock.

different elevations. They are wedged between the coast range and the Andes Mountains. The high basins are in northern Chile. Andean streams have partially filled them with rock debris of past geologic ages. Along the Andean edge of the valley, waterborne gravel and coarse sand form huge, gently sloping alluvial fans at the base of the eroding mountains.

Andean streams have carried smaller size sediments—fine sands, clays, and salts—down the alluvial fans and deposited them in basin floors. These deposits form a crust of a rare salt-bearing mineral. Since the nineteenth century, mining operations have extracted sodium nitrate, a valuable mineral for the manufacture of gunpowder and fertilizer, from the deposits. The valley's Andean edge has silver, gold, and copper ore deposits. The deposits of copper are so huge that Chile is the world's leading producer of this metal. Copper and nitrate mining camps are an important basis for settlement in Chile's desert north.

Water, like mining, has a primary influence on settlement. Because streams are usually dry in the north, wells are dug into the ground to tap into aquifers (porous layers of rock) that store Andean water. Mining operations, mining towns and camps, and small agricultural communities depend on this groundwater and the water of intermittent streams.

The Central Valley basins in middle Chile are lower in elevation than those in the north. Andean rivers with permanent, year-round flows have filled these basins with deep, nutrient-rich layers of alluvium. The Aconcagua River drains the northernmost basin; the Bío Bío River drains the southernmost depression. As you will see in coming chapters, this relatively small area of Chile, aided by its mild climate, Andean water supply, and fertile alluvial soils, is the nation's chief farming region and main population, economic, cultural, and political center.

The Central Valley of southern Chile is south of the Bío Bío River. The valley floor is closest to sea level there. Geographers call most of this area the Lakes District, because hundreds of small rivers and streams descend from the Andes to form lakes, some quite large, in the lower elevations. Andean glaciers of the Ice Age are responsible for the lakes. They eroded rock material from the eastern mountains and carried the debris into the valley. End moraines (mounds of material the size of small hills left by glaciers) dam the streams to form the lakes. The undulating surface of lake-filled basins, pastures, and low, forest-covered moraines forms a picturesque landscape. The natural beauty of this area makes it a popular destination for tourists, mainly Chileans and Argentines who visit the area during the summer.

WEATHER AND CLIMATE

Chile's climates include a hot, parched desert—the Atacama—in the north, a Mediterranean climate in the middle, a marine (ocean-influenced) climate in the south, and a tundra (subpolar) climate in the extreme south. Temperatures decrease at increasingly higher latitudes (Table 1).

Table 1: Average Annual Temperatures of Coastal Locations

LOCATION	LATITUDE	TEMPERATURE °F (°C)
Arica	18° S	67 (19)
Antofagasta	23° S	63 (17)
Valparaíso	33° S	58 (14)
Concepción	36° S	55 (13)
Valdivia	39° S	54 (12)
Puerto Montt	41° S	51 (11)
Puerto Aisén	45° S	48 (9)
Punta Arenas	53° S	44 (7)

Chileans refer to the Atacama Desert as *El Norte Grande* (The Big North). A dry, subtropical, high-pressure air mass sits stubbornly over the area all year. As a result, the region receives less than 10 inches (250 millimeters) of precipitation. In the lowlands, precipitation only occurs in the summer

(December through February) when rare, but occasionally fierce, thundershowers take place. The Atacama Desert is renowned as the world's driest desert. Arica has the world's lowest average annual precipitation, a scant 0.03 inches (0.762 millimeters).

Nearby Iquique holds the record for the number of uninterrupted years without even a trace of rain: 14. Enough winter snow falls in the peaks of the Andes to provide stream runoff for farming in isolated oases in the low desert. The streams, however, are ephemeral, meaning that they run for only short periods. After a rain, the water comes to a stop, evaporates, or seeps into the streambed and disappears. The Loa River is the only stream with a permanent flow. It is large enough to flow from the Andes across the desert to the ocean.

Chileans refer to the semiarid zone on the southern fringe of the Atacama Desert as *El Norte Chico* (The Little North). This zone is a transition from the arid desert to the more humid climates of central and southern Chile. A small amount of rainfall occurs in the winter, June through August, when leftovers of Pacific cyclonic storms arrive. Several small rivers (the Copiapó, Huasco, Elqui, Choapa, and Acongcagua) manage to meander to the seashore. The arrival of these storms is unreliable, so droughts occur every few years. Streams often dry up, much to the dismay of farmers and ranchers.

Middle Chile has a Mediterranean climate. This type of climate also exists around the shore of the Mediterranean Sea (hence the name) and in California, South Africa, and Australia. Mediterranean climates have mild, wet winters and dry summers. Chile's Mediterranean climate extends from the port city of Valparaíso, which is at the mouth of the Aconguaga River, to slightly south of the Bío Bío River. In winter, the edge of the same subtropical high-pressure air mass that dominates northern Chile shifts slightly north (toward the equator) and away from middle Chile. The winter shift allows eastward-moving cyclonic storms from the Pacific to pass over the region.

Because of mild temperatures, virtually all of the precipitation comes as rain. In summer, December through February, the edge of the high-pressure air mass shifts south (toward the pole), over middle Chile and slightly beyond to Puerto Montt. This shift forces the Pacific cyclonic storms farther south and causes a dry summer. Rare thunderstorms bring brief periods of relief to the dryness of summer. They also bring the threat of forest fires in the Andes from lightning strikes.

The coast range affects middle Chile's Mediterranean climate. It forms a barrier that blocks the cool summer breeze off the Pacific, making the summer temperatures on the coast cooler than those in the Central Valley. As a result, Santiago, which is in the valley, averages 16 days each summer with temperatures greater than 90 °F (32 °C), whereas Concepción, on the coast, has never recorded a temperature in the nineties. The coast range also impedes moisture-bearing winter winds blowing from the ocean. As a result, there is a "rain shadow" of low precipitation in the Central Valley. The coastal areas receive about 40 to 50 inches (1,000 to 1,300 millimeters), whereas Santiago, located in the valley, receives only 11 inches (280 millimeters) annually.

The high elevations of middle Chile's central Andes are too wet and cold to have a Mediterranean climate. Because of the elevation, precipitation is greater than 100 inches (2,500 millimeters) in some places, and it comes mainly in the form of snow. In fact, transportation routes through the mountain passes are typically closed in the winter due to heavy snowstorms. The only all-season route to Argentina is the *Los Libertadores* (The Liberators) tunnel northeast of Santiago. As previously mentioned, snowfall above about 8,000 feet (3,500 meters) is sufficient to support the existence of glaciers in this part of the Andes.

Southern Chile has a marine (ocean-influenced) climate. Precipitation from Pacific cyclonic storms occurs there year-round. The storms form as a cold polar and warm tropical air mix and spiral violently upward over the Pacific Ocean. Southern Chile is cool and wet as the storms pass over land. In the north end of southern Chile, temperatures are mildest in part because of the moderating influence of the ocean. The seaport of Puerto Montt represents the north-end climate. The city has an average annual temperature of 51 °F (10 °C) and an annual precipitation level of 86 inches (2,184 millimeters).

Precipitation totals in southern Chile vary greatly from place to place. The coastal islands have some of the heaviest precipitation in South America. The cloud-shrouded islands of Madre de Dios *(Mother of God)* and Wellington receive about 275 inches (7000 millimeters). The western side of the Andes gets more than 120 inches (2,500 millimeters), which is more typical for the region. In stark contrast, the eastern side is in a rain shadow and gets less than 20 inches (500 millimeters) in some places.

In the extreme south (which includes the Patagonian Andes and Tierra del Fuego), short winter days and low sun angles keep temperatures low. Pacific Ocean waters of the frigid Antarctic Current and cold Humboldt Current cut temperatures more. Fierce winds make the temperatures feel even colder. Despite relatively low elevations, snow from frequent cyclonic storms creates massive ice fields in the Patagonian Andes. In contrast, on the island of Tierra del Fuego, a rain shadow cuts precipitation to a drizzle. Here, moisture often hangs in the air as a drippy fog. Punta Arenas, the main settlement in the extreme south, receives only 16 inches (406 millimeters) of precipitation, but the dampness of clouds and fog is everywhere. The average annual temperature is just 44 °F (7 °C).

The cold Humboldt Current plays an important role in the climate of coastal Chile. The current is born as it splits from the eastward-traveling Antarctic Current and turns north to pass next to Chile. The Humboldt warms up as it flows toward the equator, but it remains cool enough to affect summer temperatures along the coasts of middle and northern Chile. As subtropical heat is drawn into the cold current, air temperatures decrease and a soupy fog forms offshore. The fog is so thick that Chileans and Peruvians call it a *garúa*, which means "drizzle" in Spanish. A sea breeze blows the cool air and the garúa onshore, bringing relief from summer temperatures there. This moderating effect does not extend inland; the coast range blocks the cool sea breeze and garúa, except where there are valley openings. The resulting difference between inland and coastal temperatures in the summer is noteworthy. For example, daytime temperatures in January in inland Santiago average 85 °F (29 °C), whereas in coastal Concepción, they average 71° F (22 °C). As we will see, the cold Humboldt Current's affect on summer temperatures is significant enough to affect patterns of natural vegetation and agriculture in the country.

PLANTS AND SOILS

In northern Chile, plant life is sparse because of poor soils, desert dryness, and harsh temperatures. A few species of grass survive the scarcity of soil moisture by growing in bunches. The grasses provide some forage for grazing cattle, sheep, mules, llamas, and other camel-like livestock. A few cacti species also survive the desert conditions. The lowest part of the basin floors is barren because the soil is too salty for plants to grow. Between the basin floors and the bases of alluvial fans, the tamarugo tree once covered hundreds of square miles. The tree grew to a height of 80 feet (25 meters), and its deep roots reached the Andean groundwater below. The tamarugo is almost extinct now. The abundance of such a tall tree in a desert must have been a fantastic scene for early inhabitants and explorers of the region. By the beginning of the twentieth century, most of the tamarugo trees had been cut down and the wood used for fuel in foundries that processed copper and sodium nitrate. Trees were also lost because ranchers allowed sheep and cattle to eat the pulpy seedpods. As a result, the tamarugo was unable to reproduce in large numbers.

Northern Chile has two other interesting plants. The green, resinous, fragrant tola bush grows wherever Andean groundwater seeps to the surface. In mountain canyons, there are small groves of the queñoa tree. The tree can be 10 to 13 feet (3 to 4 meters) in height. Its trunk and branches appear dry and twisted, but its tiny leaves conserve moisture.

The Mediterranean climate in middle Chile is much better than the desert for plant growth and soil development. The soils are deep and fertile in the Central Valley. Andean streams have added alluvium and, volcanic eruptions have added layers of mineral-rich ash. In order to take advantage of the soil fertility, Chileans have removed natural vegetation from the valley floor and Andean foothills to grow crops and graze animals. On steeper slopes in the foothills, where farming is too difficult, a mixture of shrubs and oak and pine trees still thrives. Ascending into the main part of the Andes, decreasing temperatures limit plant growth. Only pine trees do well there. At 8,000 feet (2,400 meters), temperatures are so cold that only a few scraggly pines, widely spaced shrubs, and bunch grasses survive. Above 8,000 feet (2,400 meters), only mosses, lichens, and annual flowering plants can cling to life.

In southern Chile, a dense mid-latitude rain forest, composed of broadleaf, evergreen species, covers the area's islands and lower mountain slopes. This rain forest has fewer trees and less dense growth of underbrush compared to the tropical rain forest. In small areas of scattered, mixed woodlands, two unique trees appear together here and in neighboring areas of Argentina. The first is the deciduous southern beech. The second is the evergreen araucaria pine. The araucaria's nuts are a traditional dietary staple of Indians in this part of South America. Both trees are harvested for their timber today.

Because of the differences in climate throughout Chile, the animal life also varies. The coastal areas feature bird life such as penguins and Chile's national bird, the Andean condor, while southern areas feature more marine life. Members of the South American camelid family, including llamas, seen here grazing in the shadow of the volcano, inhabit the northern Andes.

FAUNA

Fauna (animal life) also varies from north to south. The list of interesting mammals is endless, including many fur-bearing animals that are endangered because of a long history of over-hunting. In the northern Andes are all four members of the South American camelid family: the llama, alpaca, vicuña, and guanaco. These camel-like animals are hard to tell apart. The llama and alpaca are longhaired and valued for their wool. For that reason, they are tamed and held in corrals most of the time.

The large *huemul* deer, like the four camelids, graze in herds. The huemul is found in many different habitats of Chile, but it is an endangered species because of overhunting. This handsome deer appears on the Chilean coat of arms. The southern forests shelter the Darwin fox, another endangered species. The tiny *pudú*, which is the world's smallest deer and another endangered species, survives on Chiloé Island and a nearby island. Chile also has several kinds of marsupials, or animals with pouches like that of a kangaroo or opossum. Elusive Andean wolves, wildcats, and pumas prey on all these animals. The *vizcacha* is also an Andean dweller. It looks like a large rabbit, but it is a rodent and a relative of the Chilean guinea pig and chinchilla, which are also Andean inhabitants.

Coastal areas teem with all kinds of bird life: seagulls, pelicans, petrels, and penguins. Sea swallows and cormorants are also abundant. Inland, Chilean flamingos busy them-selves by probing the mud of altiplano lakes for snails and bugs in winter. Like brush strokes of pink, they streak across the sky on their way to southern Chile in the summer. Other inland birds—swallows, woodpeckers, hummingbirds, doves, and ducks—occupy the many niches of Chile's crazy-quilt geography. The giant Andean condor, Chile's national bird, occasionally is seen in the mountains. In Tierra del Fuego, this vulture preys on the sheep population. Chile also has penguins. This flightless bird lives in scattered coastal colonies. Each colony has several thousand members. Most penguins spend the entire year in southern Chile, but in winter, some of them ride the Humboldt Current as far as northern Chile.

There are few species of freshwater fishes natural to Chile. The lake trout, introduced from North America, is plentiful and reaches sizes of 30 inches (76.2 centimeters) or more. A wide variety of ocean fish abound in the cool coastal waters. Chile is one of the world's largest fish exporters because of the large marine fish population. Big game fishing for marlin and swordfish is excellent near Tocopilla, north of Antofagasta. Tuna and anchovies thrive along most of the coast.

Marine mammals increase in number farther south. In the cool Humboldt Current, sea otters, seals, and sea lions are near the top of the food chain. They feed on an abundant supply of fish, shellfish, and squid. Further offshore, dolphins feed on small fish. Higher on the food chain, orcas (killer whales) feed on the sea otters, seals, sea lions, and dolphins. Whales also frequent Chile's waters. Early whale hunters almost killed these magnificent mammals off for their oily blubber. The oil in the blubber lit many a lantern in the nineteenth century. In the twentieth century, whale oil became more important as a lubricant and as an ingredient in cosmetics, among other things. Some whales, such as the minke, also became favored for their meat. Blue whales are probably the most prominent (and most interesting) in Chilean waters. They are now protected from overhunting. They have unique baleen plates instead of teeth. They troll the water with their mouths open and use the plates to filter out zooplankton (microscopic animals) for their food.

FOREST AND WILDLIFE PROTECTION

Chile has some beautiful wilderness areas where laws protect wildlife and vegetation. Wilderness areas are also remote areas, and as a result, humans sneak into these areas to cut valuable trees for timber and to hunt wild animals, such as the huemul. The huemul and several other species of land mammals are prized for their meat and hides. Because of poaching, such animals are on the verge of extinction. Almost one-fifth of Chile is protected to varying degrees in national parks and reserves.

Chile's diverse physical geography means that its national treasures are extremely varied. The national forestry commission administers 32 national parks, 47 national reserves, and 13 natural monuments. Chileans are making efforts to preserve their forests and wildlife, because they realize that plants and animals are important resources for the future. This realization is part of Chile's historical development, which is the subject of the next chapter.

3

Chile Through Time

C hile's remote location has influenced much of its history. Indigenous peoples of the area lived on the distant fringe of the Inca civilization. Stretching from what is now Ecuador to middle Chile, the Inca Empire preceded the Spanish Empire in the Andes region. The Incas conquered Chile's northern natives and most of the natives occupying middle Chile. Under Spanish colonial rule, Chile was a neglected outpost on the edge of mineral-rich Peru and Bolivia. As an independent nation, the country has relied on far-off external powers— Britain in the nineteenth century and the United States ever since—for trade and economic progress. Nevertheless, Chile's isolation contributed to a stable society. In turn, this stability has led to the development of one of Latin America's most successful democratic nations.

INDIGENOUS PEOPLES

Several groups of indigenous peoples, or Indians, with differing customs and economies inhabited the region that is now Chile. In northern Chile, the Chango Indians occupied the coastal desert from Arica to the Choapa River. They were a nomadic people who depended on fishing from sealskin canoes for their main food supply. They also collected shellfish, hunted wild game, and gathered seeds, berries, and nuts on the marine terraces of the coast range. Farther inland were the Aymara Indians, who were sedentary, meaning they lived in permanent villages. In canyons that cut into the western edge of the altiplano, the Aymaras dug irrigation ditches and grew maize (corn), kidney beans, quinoa (a native grain), and squashes. On the edge of the altiplano, other Aymara villages grew potatoes and grazed flocks of llamas. Farther south, beyond the Loa River, Atacameño peoples practiced a similar way of life on alluvial fans and in nearby Andean canyons. In Chile's semi-arid region, the sedentary Diaguita tribe occupied villages, grew crops, and grazed llamas and alpacas next to the permanent streams that cut across the Central Valley. Altogether, about 80,000 natives lived in northern Chile at the time of the Spanish conquest.

Araucanian tribes occupied middle Chile, the Lakes District, and Chiloé Island. The tribes spoke the same language, but had different livelihoods. The Picunche were settled in the northern part of middle Chile. More advanced than the other groups, they lived in large permanent villages and built small irrigation canals for their crops. The Mapuche occupied the southern part of middle Chile and the northern Lakes District. The Huilliche Indians lived separately in the Lakes District, south of the Bío Bío River. The Mapuche and Huilliche were shifting cultivators. They lived in small villages made up of three to eight huts (*rukas*) with one household (consisting of one or more families) sharing a hut. The dwellings were usually dispersed in valleys along streams.

As shifting cultivators, the Mapuche and Huilliche burned small areas of forest near their villages to grow crops. Clearing the natural

Many groups of indigenous people inhabited Chile centuries ago, living on the fringes of the Inca civilization. One group, the Mapuche Indians, lived in the southern end of middle Chile as shifting cultivators, meaning at times the tribe would relocate to be near more fertile fields. Here, modern Mapuche Indians gather in Santiago for the signing of the "Citizen Respect Pact," which focuses funds on the development of indigenous communities in Chile.

vegetation allowed life-giving sunlight to reach the crops. Just as important, the resulting ash added nutrients (plant food) to the soil. The crops used up soil nutrients in just three or four years, so the natives had to burn new fields elsewhere. This process would be repeated every few years and resulted in the occasional relocation of villages to be closer to the increasingly distant fields. The Picunche, Mapuche, and Huilliche Indians grew crops, including maize, kidney beans, squashes, quinoa, chili peppers, and white potatoes. They also raised llamas for meat and wool and developed highly skilled pottery and textile weaving techniques.

A fourth Araucanian tribe was the Cuncos. This group depended mainly on fishing and gathering shellfish. They inhabited the island of Chiloé and nearby mainland shores. The Araucanian cultural area was small, but it had a benign climate, fertile land, and abundant resources that supported a large number of people. Estimates of the total Araucanian population at the time the Spaniards arrived range from 500,000 to 1,500,000. A common language and high population density promoted much trade and interaction among the Araucanian tribes.

South of Chiloé, numerous small populations in the Chilean archipelago managed to survive through hunting, gathering, and fishing. Unlike the Araucanian tribes, the southern indigenous groups were nomadic, meaning they moved their villages repeatedly. They had different languages, and they were more divided culturally. They included the Chono, Alacaluf, and Yámana (or Yahgan) tribes. They lived on fish and the resources of the rainforest. Two additional nomadic groups—the Tehuelche and Ona tribes—lived in Chilean Patagonia and Tierra del Fuego, respectively.

SPANISH CONQUEST AND COLONIAL PERIOD (1541–1810)

The Spaniard Francisco Pizarro conquered what is now Peru and northwestern Bolivia, the main area of the Inca Empire, in 1532–1533. The king of Spain rewarded Pizarro for his conquests by placing him in charge of this area and any additional lands that he might conquer. Pizarro was too busy founding Lima (Peru) and amassing Incan gold and silver for shipment to Spain to conquer more land. He assigned the task of conquering Chile to Pedro de Valdivia.

In 1540, seeking slaves and gold, Valdivia led his expedition from southern Peru into Chile. He met little resistance from

Chile's northern Indians. As Valdivia advanced, he captured the natives and sent most of them to work as slaves in the silver and gold mines of Bolivia. He went as far as middle Chile, where he defeated the northernmost Araucanian tribe, the Picunche Indians, and founded the town of Santiago in 1541. Six months later, the Mapuche Indians attacked from the south and nearly wiped out the settlement. The Spaniards held on, and six years later, their numbers had grown to several hundred. Although Valdivia found small amounts of gold, he realized Chile would have to be an agricultural colony. As a result, he started the Spanish policy of keeping captured Araucanian Indians as agricultural laborers rather than sending them to mines in Bolivia. The Spanish Crown appointed Valdivia the first governor of Chile for his efforts, but he was killed by the Mapuche in 1553. By then, however, he had founded the important settlements of Concepción, Valdivia, and Villarica. These southern outposts protected middle Chile from Indian attacks and enabled the development of a future Chilean society there.

The Spaniards, and Chileans after them, became deadlocked in a guerrilla war against the natives for the next three centuries. The Bío Bío River, which marks the transition between the rain forest to the south and scrub vegetation to the north, became the line separating the two cultures. The Araucanians were mobile, ready to fight, and familiar with the forest. The Spaniards and Chileans found out that these factors made subduing the native peoples difficult.

Middle Chile was cut off to the north by desert, to the south by the hostile Araucanian Indians, to the east by the Andes Mountains, and to the west by the Pacific Ocean. In addition to the area's isolation, it lacked valuable metals. Nevertheless, Spanish settlers were drawn there. The area's fertile soil and attractive climate reminded them of southern Spain, the area from which most of them had come. Middle Chile was soon divided among the Spaniards into large agricultural or pastoral estates (*latifundios*). The owners of these estates created an aristocracy, or wealthy ruling class. Those who wanted wealth in the form of gold went elsewhere.

The early colonial society that developed in middle Chile was similar to that of other Spanish colonies. There were three main social groups. The most privileged group consisted of the Spaniards who owned the large landed estates. This group included the *peninsulares* and *criollos*. The peninsulares were Spaniards born in Spain, which is part of the Iberian Peninsula, hence the name. The Spanish Crown reserved all important government jobs and other positions of influence for this group. Criollos were Spaniards born in America. Colonial policy forbade them from holding important public offices. Both subgroups could legally own land and other property, including African slaves.

Mestizos made up the group that held the middle position in society. A mestizo is a person whose heritage includes Spanish and Indian backgrounds. Because few Spanish women came to the New World, Spanish men, especially those of the lower classes, married or had informal sexual relationships with Indian women. The resulting mestizo children soon out-numbered the Indian population, because many of the natives died through epidemics, forced labor abuses, and warfare. Unlike in Peru and Bolivia, where the Indian population remained the majority, in Chile the mestizo group quickly grew to outnumber all the other groups. At the bottom of the social ladder were a few African slaves and the shrinking population of American Indians.

According to the Spanish Crown, Indians were supposed to provide labor for Spaniards. The Crown devised the *encomienda* system for this purpose. The system allowed an individual Spaniard to use natives for labor in a particular area. In return, the Spaniard, with help from Catholic missionaries, was supposed to give the natives lessons in the Spanish language and religion. (The Spaniard hardly ever kept his part of the bargain.) The Spaniards developed an encomienda system in northern Chile (then part of Peru). In middle Chile, however, there were few natives because of interracial mixing. As a result, Spaniards had to employ mestizos. Landless and homeless, mestizos soon became cowboys (ranch hands) and tenant farmers (*inquilinos* in Chilean terminology) on estates. The estate owner gave the inquilinos little or no pay for their labor. He did give them permission to build a small family cabin, to graze the few livestock they were able to own, and to cultivate a small garden. As the mestizo population grew, more and more of them became part of a floating landless population that served as day laborers in harvest or other times of peak labor demand.

INDEPENDENCE MOVEMENTS

Chile sought to break ties with Spain for the same reasons that the rest of the Spanish colonies did. First, throughout the Spanish Empire there had been a growing hostility between the American-born criollos and the peninsular Spaniards. The latter controlled the political lives of the former. The Crown would only appoint a peninsular Spaniard to be a governor, judge, mayor, tax collector, and so on. Nor could peninsular and American-born Spaniards legally intermarry. The Crown supported this separation because it feared that criollos had a bond with the land in which they had been born. Such a bond, the Crown reasoned, weakened criollos' allegiance to Spain. The only way to preserve the empire was to deny them access to political power. This policy led criollos to the irreversible conclusion that only independence from Spain would give them political rights equal to their peninsular cousins.

A second reason Spanish colonies sought independence was the criollo merchants' resentment of Spain's rigid mercantilist trading system. In such a system, colonies had to ship products directly to the mother country, not anywhere else, not even if the merchant could sell his products at a better price.

To avoid illegal smuggling, the Spanish Crown required that merchants transport all products through government customs houses on their way to and from the colony. Government agents collected taxes on the products at the customs houses. In South America, all exports and imports had to go through the customs house in Lima, Peru (or Buenos Aires, Argentina, beginning in 1778). Criollo merchants felt that the Crown's burdensome taxing system was holding back economic growth in the colonies. They also knew that direct shipments to the closest colonial ports would reduce transport costs and thereby raise profits. In Chile, the merchants wanted to use the port of Valparaíso for shipments of goods.

The intellectual climate in Europe and European colonies was a third reason for independence movements among Spanish colonies. The American colonies' independence from Great Britain and the French Revolution's spirit of equality caused colonists to question the right of Spain to control their affairs. Moreover, events in Europe were weakening Spain's control of its colonies. Spain made an alliance with France. Together, the two countries declared a costly and an ill-fated war against Great Britain in 1804. The French, under the leadership of Napoleon Bonaparte, invaded Spain in 1808. The Spanish king, Charles IV, was taken out the country by the French and put under house arrest. Napoleon placed his bother Joseph on the Spanish throne. Napoleon's unseating of the Spanish king gave Spanish American colonists a political excuse to seek independence from Spain. Up until then, many colonists had reasoned that their allegiance was to the Spanish king. Now, with the Spanish Crown under the control of a foreign power, they changed their allegiance to establishing independent nations.

NINETEENTH CENTURY INDEPENDENCE, STABILITY, AND NATION-BUILDING

Several rebel armies united to force Spain from South America in the early nineteenth century. Chile's war of Independence

Bernardo O'Higgins, sometimes known as the George Washington of Chile, led rebels to victory in Chile's War of Independence with Spain that lasted from 1810–1818. O'Higgins became dictator of Chile after the war, and strengthened the nation by forming a navy, improving cities, opening schools, and promoting trade and agriculture, before being sent into exile by his political rivals in 1823.

lasted from 1810 to 1818. A combined force of Chilean and Argentine rebels liberated the country. The rebels were under the leadership of the Chilean Bernardo O'Higgins and the Argentine General José de San Martín. O'Higgins, who had an Irish father and Spanish mother, became dictator of Chile from 1818 to 1823. Determined to strengthen Chile as a nation, he built a navy, improved cities, promoted trade and agriculture, and opened public schools and libraries. He also prohibited bullfights, because they offended British merchants, Chile's new partners in foreign trade. In 1823, Chile became the first Spanish American country to abolish slavery. In the same year, O'Higgins's political rivals forced him to give up power and go into exile in Lima, Peru. Chileans often refer to Bernardo O'Higgins as the George Washington of their country.

Chile was a success story among former Spanish colonies by the mid-nineteenth century. The country's one central cluster of people gave it a distinct plus in nation building. Unlike the other colonies, disputes and political rivalries involved a single, compact region. Thus, diplomacy was more effective in solving problems. What is more, landowning aristocrats lived on their estates, enabling them to take part in the life of rural communities. Their presence and paternal role narrowed the social gap between themselves and the large class of landless mestizo peasants. Chile's stability was unusual among South American countries. Most countries had periodic outbursts of interregional warfare and wealthy landowners usually resided in cities.

Diego Portales dominated politics from 1830 until his murder in 1837. He was never president, but he ruled from behind the scenes as a cabinet minister. He achieved his objectives by using dictatorial powers, censoring the press, and controlling elections. Although he used dubious methods to govern, his rule gave Chile a stable regime at a critical time. For almost 100 years after Portales's rule, the country enjoyed a series of presidents who served out their terms. This fact reflects the political stability that the country enjoyed. In contrast, civil wars and political assassinations were destabilizing most South American countries during the same period.

Adding to Chile's stability and the Chileans' growing identity as a nation were two wars that the country fought and won during the nineteenth century. From 1836 to 1839, Chile fought a war against the Peruvian-Bolivian Confederation. Chile was afraid that the merger of these two countries would threaten its security and stability. The victory left Peru and Bolivia as separate nations once again. From 1879 to 1884, the War of the Pacific (also known as the Chile-Peruvian War) erupted. Chile was pitted against its former rivals, Peru and Bolivia. The dispute was over control of the nitrate fields in the Atacama Desert. At the time, Chile's northern border was farther south than it is today, so that the nitrate ores lay inside Peru and Bolivia. Chilean companies and workers, however, did most of the mining. Chile's victory pushed the country's northern border to its present position and increased its national territory by one-third. The new border shut off Bolivia from direct access to the Pacific, leaving it landlocked. Taken together, Chile's two war victories made the country the dominant military and commercial power along South America's west coast.

Chile as a nation became even stronger as the government brought outlying regions under control. The country's triumph in the War of the Pacific secured its northern region. A treaty with the Mapuche natives in 1881 finally brought the southern region under Chilean rule. The country's transportation network also expanded outward from Santiago, literally tying the periphery (outer regions) to the center. William Wheelwright, an American industrialist, adopted Chile as his new home. In 1840, he created the first steamship line, which ran between Valparaíso and Panama. He also built the country's first railroad in 1851, connecting the mining centers of Caldera and Copiapó. Wheelwright also oversaw construction of the first telegraph line between Santiago and Valparaíso. These were the first links in an expanding trade and communication system that helped Chileans from the north, middle, and south to unite as a single nation by the late nineteenth century.

Much of the nineteenth century unity and stability came from Chile's steady economic growth. Nitrates and other minerals exported from northern mines generated income for Chileans and huge tax revenues for the government. Middle Chile became an important exporter of wheat and flour. These exports went first to gold rush California and then to Great Britain. Industries, notably flour milling and breweries, grew in Santiago and Valparaíso, its trading port. The new urban factories needed laborers. Santiago grew from about 40,000 inhabitants in 1800 to more than 250,000 in 1900. Similarly, Valparaíso increased from 6,000 to 130,000.

Merchants from Great Britain became the country's primary trading partners. British companies also invested large sums of money directly in the Chilean economy, particularly in nitrate mines and railroad construction. In addition, economic prosperity attracted a modest numbers of settlers from abroad. Immigrants came from all over Europe. People also emigrated from the Middle East, Peru, and Bolivia. Some of the immigrants joined the new urban middle class. Most of them ended up as laborers in cities. A minority, mostly German immigrants in the south, succeeded in farming.

Despite Chile's progress, the nineteenth century ended on an unstable note. The economy was beginning to fail. The number of unemployed nitrate miners and landless mestizos was growing. In addition, a power struggle between the president and congress, which had been brewing since the 1830s, came to a head in 1891. Congress gradually had been asserting more and more authority over the budget and cabinet ministers. Among other things, President José Manuel Balmaceda proposed to fund new programs by raising taxes in the mining sector and cutting expenditures to the navy. His political enemies were concerned, because a narrow majority in congress appeared to support his proposals. Influential members of congress (many of whom were large landowners) and the navy organized a rebellion. This was Chile's first major revolt since 1823. The rebels defeated progovernment forces in two battles and seized the city of Santiago. Balmaceda took refuge in the Argentine embassy. He remained in the embassy until the end of his legal presidential term and committed suicide there. The government remained democratic at the end of the crisis, and a newly elected president and congress took office after the uprising. Despite the brief 1891 revolt, Chileans finished the nineteenth century with a long history of political stability. They took take pride in their representative form of government, and many looked with contempt on their more chaotic neighbors.

UPHEAVALS IN THE TWENTIETH CENTURY TO THE PRESENT

If the nineteenth century was known for its democracy and stability, the most recent century is in many ways recognized for its periodic challenges to democracy. Economic problems that had been brewing in the late nineteenth century finally boiled over at the opening of the twentieth century. Chile's economy and foreign trade depended almost solely on the nitrate mining industry, which had been in decline since the 1880s.

The first serious sign of trouble came in northern Chile. In 1907, nitrate miners organized a strike for better pay and conditions. The miners and their families traveled to Santa María de Iquique, a remote mining town, to meet with government officials in order to discuss their complaints. The government did not send emissaries to the town as it had promised. Instead, it sent troops with orders to put down the strike by force. As the strikers assembled in the town plaza and church, a barrage of gunfire killed about 200 unarmed men and women. The hail of bullets also wounded hundreds of others. This bloodbath radicalized Chilean politics. In 1912, groups of dissatisfied workers in the cities, the mines, and countryside united to form the Chilean Socialist Workers Party. After the Russian Revolution in 1917, it was the basis of the Chilean Communist Party. Up to this time, political parties simply represented opposing views held by members of the ruling class. Now, Chile's politics began to reflect the nation's long-standing but largely ignored economic and social problems.

Many of the problems lay at the feet of the aristocracy. In the last decades of the nineteenth century, the ruling class was allowing agricultural production to stagnate. It was investing money in mines and urban-based factories instead. This policy was a formula for disaster, because jobs on estates employed 75 percent of Chile's rural population. What is more, the days when the gentile landowner lived on his estate and showed compassion for the tenant workers who toiled on his land were over. Businesslike managers were now operating the estates. Meanwhile, estate owners lived in luxurious houses in Santiago. They lived a lavish urban lifestyle, formed social clubs, attended the opera, and sent their children to the finest schools in Europe. They ignored Chile's declining economy and rising poverty in the cities and mining towns as well as the country-side. Indeed, in the first decade of the twentieth century, the ruling class spent more money on the purchase of luxury items from Paris (champagne, jewels, silk, and perfume) than they did on new agricultural and industrial machinery.

Dissatisfied factory and mine workers formed trade unions in the opening decades of the twentieth century. They organized themselves to pressure the government for change. They went on labor strikes. They held rallies in the streets. Some of the rallies deteriorated into violent riots. Responding to the rising tide of social unrest, the government created the Constitution of 1925. Conservative groups in Chile believed that the government was given too much power. The result was a military coup in 1928 that gave Colonel Carlos Ibáñez dictatorial powers. This coup pushed aside Chile's democratic tradition, as would happen again in the 1970s. Ibáñez's government did not survive the Great Depression, which swept the world with the Wall Street crash in 1929. Widespread unemployment and street riots forced him to resign in 1931, and democracy was restored the next year.

From 1932 to 1973, Chile was the only country in Latin America to sustain an electoral democracy. Parties and party alliances tended to appear and disappear over time. Marxist parties led the workers, as they did in the rest of the region during this period. Chile had two prominent political camps. The Socialists and the Communist parties were in the first camp. They included liberals or leftists. Leftists wanted the state to play a greater role in social and economic improvements. They also included a minority of radical full-blooded Marxist-Leninists. These people sought an armed struggle to overthrow the government and the establishment of a one-party communist system.

The second camp was the Christian Democrat party. Christian Democrats were conservatives or rightists. Rightists had strong backing from women (who gained the right to vote in 1949) and the Catholic Church. Christian Democrats were anticommunist. Both camps shared the common goals, such as the reform of landownership and nationalization of U.S.-owned copper mines. As a result, factions of these two groups often crossed over from one camp to the other. They formed temporary political parties (left-wing or right-wing coalitions) to win elections.

For nearly 50 years, Chile went through a sustained period of democracy. Nevertheless, the country was plagued by rising inflation, dependence on foreign markets and capital, and unequal income distribution. A series of presidents formed coalitions and tried to deal effectively with Chile's problems. Solutions were difficult to find, and politics became increasingly radical. Desperate for a fresh approach, in 1970 Chileans elected a Marxist, Salvador Allende Gossens, a former physician, as president. Allende led the Popular Unity party. This party was a left-wing coalition of socialists, communists, radicals, and Christian Democrats. As a Marxist, Allende called for reforms that smacked of a socialist state similar to the former Soviet Union. He sought the state ownership (nationalization) of most private industries and banks. He also called for the state's takeover and reorganization of privately owned estate lands into collectivized farms. (The former Soviet Union organized agriculture into state-run collectivized farms in which farmers worked for the state. The state owned all land and other capital—such as tractors, animals, and houses.)

Allende was the first Marxist ever elected president in a democratic country. His government faced daunting problems. The United States government was afraid that he would turn Chile into a communist (one-party) state. What is more, Allende had convinced the Chilean congress to nationalize the U.S. copper mines, although he had not made the move to do so. Richard Nixon, the U.S. president, responded by secretly financing Allende's political opposition. Moreover, a majority of Chileans did not support his leadership. In a multicandidate race, only 36% of the electorate voted for him. There were also massive street demonstrations because of shortages in food and other consumer items. In addition, there was much talk among Allende's supporters that Chile was following a "peaceful road to socialism." Yet most Chileans and leaders of the military— who were mostly sons of the ruling class—did not want a communist-run state. Because of these factors, a military coup overthrew Allende in 1973.

General Augusto Pinochet emerged as the leader of the military government. He dissolved congress, banned leftist parties, and suspended all others. Initially, the regime kidnapped, tortured, and murdered political opponents. Gradually, the regime allowed greater freedom of assembly, speech, and association. Political parties began to function openly again in 1987. Pinochet gave up his power in 1990, after Chileans voted

Hoping to revive their slumping economy, Chileans elected Marxist Salvadore Allende, who promised many reforms, as president in 1970. However, many Chileans and leaders of the military did not support the president's Socialist governments, and Allende (seen here, right) was overthrown by General Augusto Pinochet (left) in 1973. Pinochet led a brutal regime, murdering and torturing political opponents, but he gave up his power in 1990 after being voted out of office.

him out of office. Freely elected governments have ruled Chile ever since.

Chile continues to deal with the legacy of Pinochet's brutal regime. In 1990, one of Patricio Alwin's first acts as president was to establish the National Truth and Reconciliation Commission.

The Commission's purpose is to find out what happened to members of Pinochet's political opposition. The Commission's findings have led to the arrest and prosecution of former army officers and former leaders of the Pinochet's secret police. The Commission's work eventually led to the house arrest of Pinochet himself. The Santiago appeals court closed the case in 2003. The court declared the former dictator unfit for trial for health reasons.

Tens of thousands of Chileans are still dealing with the loss of close family members torn from them by Pinochet's henchmen. Chilean artists continue to express the plight of victims in crafts, dance, paintings and theater. Without a doubt, Pinochet's brutal rule has left an indelible imprint on the people and culture of the country.

CHAPTER

4

People and Culture

Geography and history formed the crucible from which Chile was born. In the twentieth century, the country survived dictatorships and social upheavals to become a model of democracy in Latin America. Today, the vitality of its people and culture heighten the world's respect for this small nation even more.

POPULATION

Chile's 15.7 million people are descended from various ethnic groups, most of whom intermixed during the country's history. Mestizos, those of mixed European and Indian ancestry, make up 70 percent of the population. About 25 percent are European immigrants and their descendents. Most of this group has Spanish ancestors, the most privileged of whom have unmixed bloodlines traced to colonial criollo and peninsular families. Members of the indigenous groups comprise about 3 percent of the population.

Although they are relatively few in number today, American Indians are important to the nation's history and culture. The Mapuche are the most numerous group, numbering about 600,000. Most of them occupy the Araucanian Region and the Lakes Regions. There are several thousand Huilliche-speaking Indians. They still live in the Lakes Region, south of the Mapuche area. The Indian tribes of the archipelago farther south are nearly extinct. About 2,500 of the Alacaluf (Kawashkar) are the only surviving group. Another area of Indian settlement is the altiplano of the extreme north. About 50,000 Aymara Indians reside there. They are a spillover population from neighboring Bolivia, where Aymara-speakers make up one-fourth of that country's population. A group of about 20,000 Atacameñoes resides in the Central Valley and coast range in the far north.

The growth rate of the nation's general population was 1.06 percent in 2003. This percentage was lower than most other South American nations. Uruguay, Brazil, and Guyana had lower growth rates, but they also lost population because of out migration. (In today's world, a high population growth rate is not a good thing, because as the years go by, the population increasingly pressures the nation's natural resources.) Chile's average life expectancy, slightly over 76 years, is the second longest in South America (trailing only French Guiana). The high life expectancy reflects Chile's excellent national heath care system.

Eighty-seven percent of all Chileans live in cities, a marked increase of 17 percent in the last 10 years or so. About 80 percent of the nation's people live in just 20 percent of the total area—the main agricultural region of middle Chile. The most densely settled area is Metropolitan Santiago, which, with a population of nearly 6.5 million, dominates the middle region and the nation. The city itself is home to about 4.9 million Chileans. Geographers call cities such as Santiago primate cities. A primate city has a population that is more than twice that of the next largest community. It also is the country's political, economic, and cultural center. Santiago is home to the nation's largest universities and has most of its government offices, banks, insurance companies, and industries.

Middle Chile has several important cities beyond the borders of Metropolitan Santiago. Valparaíso has nearly 300,000 people. It is connected by highway and railroad to Santiago and is the capital's main seaport. Viña del Mar has a population of about 360,000 people. It is the country's main resort city and is only 6 miles (8 kilometers) from Valparaíso. Concepción has about 400,000 inhabitants. It is situated 10 miles (16 kilometers) inland, near the mouth of the Bío Bío River. The port of Talcahuano (population 300,000) serves Concepción. Most cities in middle Chile are experiencing rapid growth mostly caused by migration of people from other areas of the country who come seeking jobs.

The cities in northern and southern Chile are also increasing in size because of migration from rural areas. For the most part, the main cities are commercial seaports. Immigrants seek jobs on fishing boats. They also hope to find work at dockyards, warehouses, and processing plants. Transportation routes link the seaports to mining and agricultural towns in interior Chile. In a few cases, they link to Bolivia and Argentina. In the arid north, Antofagasta is the largest city, with about 267,000 people. Also important are Arica and Iquique, both with about 200,000 people. There are no large cities in the northern desert interior. Temuco (259,000) is the largest city in southern Chile. The two major seaport centers in southern Chile are Puerto Montt (168,000) and Punta Arenas (131,000). Of the world's cities, only Argentina's Ushuaia lies farther south than Punta Arenas.

MESTIZO MELTING POTS

Chileans are primarily mestizos, the product of unions between the country's indigenous peoples and various European colonizers. Demographers (scientists who study populations) call areas where people of diverse racial and cultural backgrounds "co-mingle melting pots." The Chilean people and culture evolved from four major melting pots: the Central Valley, the Araucania Region, the Lakes Region, and the Magallanes

Region. Most mestizos in these regions have Spanish and Indian ancestors. Each region includes a unique mixture of other European ancestors, most of who could not speak a word of Spanish when they first arrived. Today, these regions offer slightly different flavors of Chilean culture.

Spanish colonialists concentrated their settlements in middle Chile. Thus, this region was by far the largest European group in the country's formative years. Therefore, the Spanish cultural influence was strongest there. Some British and Irish immigrants came during the Spanish colonial period. After independence, the region was the main entry point for virtually every other major immigrant group. Some members of these arriving groups stayed in the valley and married local Chileans. Other immigrants quickly moved out of the valley to settle an expanding frontier. Beginning in about 1860, there was a steady out migration of recently arrived foreign immigrants and mestizos to nitrate, copper, silver, and coal mines beyond the valley, mainly in northern Chile. Later, immigrants and mestizos pushed into the southern Lakes and Magallenas regions. In the mid-twentieth century, there was a stream of Chilean mestizos from the middle region into the Argentine oases on the eastern side of the Andes.

A second melting pot was in the Araucania region, an area between the Central Valley and the Lakes Region, near the town of Temuco. The Araucania Region is the heartland of the Mapuche Indians. The Mapuches were the only major Araucanian tribe to survive Spanish colonization and the ensuing Indian wars. To make room for European settlers, the Chilean government established a reservation policy in 1866, which moved most of the remaining Mapuches onto reservations. These reservations are in the hills to the south and west of Temuco. They are still home to the Mapuche culture. About 200,000 Mapuche who live in this region are active speakers of the Mapuche language. Many Mapuche people, pressed by the need for work, have moved to the cities where they have gradually lost their cultural identity. By

1890, small groups of Boers (Dutch colonists from southern Africa), Italians, French, and Swiss immigrants had settled this area. Mestizos from northern and middle Chile were also drawn to the region. Generally uneducated and destitute, they were seeking to make a new start in what was then a settlement frontier.

Immigrants also helped form a third melting pot in the Lakes Region. In the nineteenth century, the Chilean government actively sought more European colonists to settle this part of the frontier. German immigration began in 1848 and lasted for 90 years. By 1900, 30,000 Germans had cleared the forest, planted crops, and founded small towns. Many German men married Indian women there. The resulting German mestizos and other Indians mixed with Chilean mestizos who entered the region from middle Chile. Today, the cities of Valdivia, Llanquihue, Osorno, and Puerto Montt, and fishing villages of northern Chiloé, have a strong German influence in architecture, food, and culture. What is more, German surnames are still common, as is the German language.

Magallanes, the southernmost region of the country, was another melting pot of diverse peoples. Large-scale immigration occurred from 1845 to 1906. Among the earliest arrivals were Chilotes (Chileans from Chiloé Island). Afterward, British businessmen started sheep *estancias* (ranches) in the grassy parts of Patagonia and Tierra del Fuego. They raised merino sheep for their mutton and fine wool. Laborers for the estancias included Chileans migrants. Nearly as many foreign migrants came as well. The latter were mostly from Eastern Europe, particularly Croatia. Croatians and their descendents still make up a large fraction of Magallanes' population. In Punta Arenas, one in four residents is of Croatian decent. Chile's Croatian population is the fifth largest in the world. Immigrants also arrived from Spain, Great Britain, Italy, Germany, Serbia, Bosnia and Herzegovina, Argentina, and France during the late nineteenth and early twentieth centuries.

Chile is a melting pot, and many of its people are mestizos, or products of marriage between indigenous peoples and Europeans. Germans are one European group that flooded the Lakes Region in the nineteenth century. Today, German surnames are still common in the area, and German influence can be found in the culture, food, and architecture, as evidenced by this house in Valdivia.

Immigration added Middle Easterners to the melting pots. They came in two groups. The first group started arriving in the second half of the nineteenth century. They were seeking to escape from turmoil in the Middle East caused by the Crimean War. This war pitted Great Britain against the Turkish Ottoman Empire. The Turks were forcing male Palestinians, Syrians, and Lebanese, especially those who were Christians, to become soldiers in the war. At the time, the Chilean government was seeking settlers for its southern region. Parents put their adult sons on boats bound for Chile so they would not have to fight in the war. The second grouping of Middle Easterners was primarily Palestinian families from the area of Bethlehem. They began arriving in 1948, after the creation of the state of Israel. Chilean society absorbed the Middle Easterners, many of whom became productive members of the business community and the government. There are about 300,000 people of Middle Eastern origin living in Chile today.

LANGUAGE AND RELIGION

Most Chileans share a common language and religion. Spanish is the official language of Chile. Except for small minorities of Indians and Germans, everyone speaks the language. The Spanish word for the language is *español*. Guillermo Castillo-Feliâu, author of *Culture and Customs of Chile*, points out that in Chile, as well as most other countries of Spanish America, people prefer to say *castellano*, rather than español. He notes that to say, "Do you speak Spanish?" one normally says "*Habla castellan?*" Spanish-speaking South Americans prefer saying the latter, because the Spanish language of South America is so different from that of Spain. Some observers even think of Chilean Spanish as a separate language, because the Spanish spoken in Chile is such a great mixture of languages. Chileans make liberal usage of words from American Indian, English, German, Italian, and even Serbo-Croatian languages. What is more, Chileans' pronunciation of many Spanish words is very different from the Spanish spoken in neighboring countries.

Like the rest of Spanish America, Chile has been Roman Catholic since its beginnings in the early 1500s. During colonial times, the Church and the Crown were essentially a partnership. Their common objective was to colonize new lands and to convert Indians to Christianity. For example, if an area had a relatively large population, the Crown decreed that the Spanish conquistadors must establish churches there. In return, the Church would teach scripture to the Indians and keep colonists faithful to the Spanish king because he was, supposedly, divinely inspired. The Crown and Church considered a marriage between a Spaniard and an Indian or a Spaniard and a mestizo disloyal acts. The purer a Spaniard's bloodline, the more faithful he or she would be to God and country, or so the reasoning went. The Crown attempted to discourage interracial nuptials by giving lucrative and prestigious government jobs only to Spaniards born and married in Spain.

There were fewer Indians and hardly any African slaves in Chile compared to other Spanish colonies. Thus, the Church was able to spend more time ministering to the Spanish colonists. The Crown and Church tried to keep a monopoly on Christianity by allowing only Spanish citizens to migrate to Chile. In this way, Spain kept away Europeans who belonged to other Christian religions until the nineteenth century, when important changes began to occur. Immigrants from other parts of Europe, especially Great Britain and Germany, were entering its colonies. British settlers brought their Anglican faith. German immigrants brought either Roman Catholicism or Lutheranism to their new home. Anglicans and Lutherans did not attempt to preach beyond the immigrants' settlements, however. In Chile, the Roman Catholic Church was permitting the union of German Lutherans and mestizo Chilean Catholics by 1880. Protestant missionaries from the United States, who preached their beliefs to anyone who would listen, were entering Chile. All the while, the government gave financial support to the Catholic Church. The Church, in turn, tended to support politicians who wanted to keep the conservative, aristocratic elite in power.

Chile's 1925 constitution officially disbanded the alliance between the Roman Catholic Church and the state. The constitution recognized the free exercise of all religions. It gave other religious groups the right to own property and to erect churches. Moreover, the government would no longer provide financial support to the Church. In the following decades, the Catholic Church gradually became a religious body that better represented Chilean society as a whole. Today, it no longer allies itself automatically with conservative elements of the government. Chile's Roman Catholics generally respect the rules of the Church, but many members reject some of the conservative views of the Vatican. Many, for example, practice birth control. Many also support marriage of the clergy and, to some extent, abortion.

The number of Roman Catholics has been declining since 1970. At the same time, the Protestant population has been increasing. About 90 percent of Chile's total population was Roman Catholic in 1970. Slightly more than 6 percent was Protestant at the time. The 1992 census shows that 77 percent of the population declared itself Roman Catholic. The number of Protestants more than doubled between 1970 and 1992, increasing from 6 to 13 percent. The increase in Protestants was primarily caused by Catholics converting to evangelical Protestant sects. Other religious groups include members of the Jewish, Muslim, and Christian Orthodox faiths.

LITERATURE AND POETRY

Chile enjoys one of the highest literacy rates in South America, just over 95 percent. Aside from the Bible, the most famous literary work among Chileans is *La Araucana*, by Alonso de Ercilla y Zúñiga, a sixteenth-century Spanish soldier turned poet. Ercillia was born in Madrid, Spain, in 1533. When he was 23 years old, he went to Lima, Peru, and joined a Spanish expeditionary force with the rank of captain. The Spanish Viceroy of Peru sent the force to Chile to fight the Araucanian Indians there. Ercillia remained in Chile for only three years (1556 to 1559). He returned to Lima and then went back to Spain, where he wrote *La Araucana*, a 3,000-verse epic poem.

Although other religions have gained popularity in recent years, Roman Catholicism is and for centuries has been the main religion of Chile. Here, pilgrims carry a statue of Chile's patron saint, the Virgin del Carmen, through the streets of La Tirana during the annual celebration to honor the saint.

Every school child reads *La Araucana*, not as much for its literary quality as for its value as a meaningful description of the birth of the new nation. Ercillia's poetic brush depicts two rival warriors—the Araucania Indian and the Spanish soldier. He describes both as heroes struggling for the same land but for different and equally noble reasons. *La Araucana* is important, because Ercillia merges the power, bravery, and character of the two heroes into a single spirit. Because Chile is a mestizo country, the poem helps Chileans define who they are as a people. Literary historians recognize Ercilla as a great poet, mainly for the brilliance of *La Araucana*. He died in Spain in 1594, at the age of 62.

Two modern Chilean poets have won the Nobel Prize for literature: Gabriela Mistral and Pablo Neruda. As Nobel Prize winners, they are major figures in Chilean, Latin American, and world literature. Gabriela Mistral (1889–1957) was a teacher in several rural elementary and secondary schools. She was a private person who lived very simply. Her private nature cloaked the sensitivity and compassion of her poetry. When Mistral was 17, she fell in love with a man who later committed suicide. Mistral's best book, *Desolación* (Desolation), published in 1922, expressed her bittersweet feelings of losing a lover. She received the Nobel Prize in 1945, making her the first Chilean, the first Spanish American, and the first woman writing in Spanish to receive the award. Mistral's life and poetry was not a matter of public controversy, so she was accepted in political circles. She became a Chilean diplomat and represented Chile as a cultural attaché in various countries of Europe and in the United States. She never married, although she adored children, and eventually settled in Roslyn, New York, where she died. Langston Hughes translated some of her poems into English in *Selected Poems of Gabriela Mistral*.

The poems of Pablo Neruda (1904–1973) often used images of the countryside and common people as his subjects, because they dealt with the human sorrows of abandonment and solitude. He received the Nobel Prize in 1971, 26 years after Mistral received the prize. (Neruda was Latin America's third recipient of the award; the second was Miguel Angel Asturias, a Guatemalan novelist, in 1967.) As a teenager, Neruda lived in the town of Temuco, where he met Mistral, who was an undiscovered poet teaching elementary school there. She encouraged his writing and at 13, he published some articles in the local daily newspaper.

Growing up, Neruda became a much more controversial figure than Mistral. He was flamboyant and liked to spend money on lavish homes. He married several times, and his private life was public knowledge. Neruda also was more combative about politics than was Mistral. He became a member of the Communist Party as an outspoken champion of the poor laborer. He won election as senator of Tarapacá and Antofagasta, the mining provinces of the Norte Grande. In 1946, because of his leftist political views, the government forced him into exile in Argentina. He escaped by foot and horseback across the southern Andes.

Neruda returned to Chile and became the Communist Party candidate for president of 1969. He ran against his old friend Salvador Allende, the Popular Unity Party's candidate. Allende won the election, but he appointed Neruda ambassador to France. Neruda received the Nobel Prize while he was in France. He died in 1973, shortly after Allende was killed in a military coup. Neruda died a rich man and left his wealth to the Chilean people through a charitable foundation. Some of his work is available in English translation, such as *Heights of Macchu Picchu, The Stones of Chile,* and *Passions and Impressions.*

Chile's most famous living writer is Isabel Allende (1942–), the niece of Salvador Allende. This fact helped her become recognized as an author. Her own talent as a writer places her among the best contemporary Latin American novelists. Her writing is fictional, but her characters teach much about the mystical qualities of people. Her early works dealt with settings and characters in Latin America. She moved to the United States after her uncle was thrown out of power in 1973. Since then, her poems have involved North America, as well as Latin America.

FINE AND PERFORMING ARTS

Chile's cultural interests extend beyond literature to include the entire range of artistic expression. Santiago contains the Palace of Fine Arts, the National Library, the National Ballet, symphony orchestras, and theater companies. The performing arts, especially dance and music, play key roles in Chile's ethnic and national identity.

The *cuenca*, which originated in the countryside, is Chile's national dance. It is a traditional part of Independence Day (September 18) celebrations. Dancers perform the cuenca in various ways depending on their regional or ethnic origins. No matter the version, it involves an aggressive, strutting male courting a shy but flattered female. Using metaphors, Castillo-Felix, author of *Culture and Customs of Chile*, imagined the dance as "a reenactment of the cock's courting of the hen, the amorous wooing of a couple, or even the attempt of a huasco [Chilean cowboy] to lasso a young mare." Typically, a male and female dance around one another, "brandishing handkerchiefs, in step to music played by instruments such as the guitar, the harp, and the accordion, as one or more singers tell a story."

Ethnic folk music includes various songs and tunes that recall lives of ordinary people plus historical events or celebrations rooted in history. The music (and dance) is evident in different forms depending on the ethnic group. It is typical music of the countryside but often appeals to the city dweller as well.

The folk band Inti Illimani (pronounced Inte-E-gee-mane in the Aymara language) is perhaps the most internationally famous Chilean group. Its music is of the classical Andean type. Andean music is unique, because it combines string instruments from other cultures with instruments that are native to South America. The string instruments include the acoustic (nonelectrical) guitar, *tipla* (a four-stringed instrument that sounds like a harpsichord), and *charango* (a mandolin-like instrument that has an armadillo shell as the sounding board). Indigenous instruments include bamboo panpipes *(zampoñas)*,

Performing arts, especially music and dance, including Chile's national dance, the *cuenca*, play an important part in the country's identity. Here, dancers and musicians perform a traditional dance in Santiago's Plaza de Armas.

the cane flute (*quena*, which is made from a hollowed out sugarcane stalk), and the turtleback-shaped *ocarina* (which is made of clay). The rain stick (*palo de lluvia*) is a dried cactus branch filled with small beads. The musician holds the instrument upright and then inverts it. The beads pour from one end of the stalk to the other to make the sound of falling rain. The tambourine (of various origins) and the *bombo* (a drum of African origin) are typical percussion instruments.

The nation's present-day music is in a parallel universe. A syrupy harmony of international pop dominates the airwaves. At the same time, a fervent, moral rhythm—"New Song"—hangs on in the background. "New Song" is a type of folk music. In the late 1960s, inspired by the hardships of poor miners, tenant farmers, and factory workers, the early lyrics protested against the bleak life and hopelessness that oppression and poverty bring. The early songs became popular among Marxists, socialists, and other groups who wanted radical changes in government. Contemporary lyrics support change, but they are less divisive and appeal to a broader range of Chileans.

The New Song music reminds people that their multicultural heritage makes them a stronger nation and that the "haves" should be willing to help the "have-nots." The turbulent politics of the 1960s gave birth to the music, and the movement reached its peak of acclaim during the Allende presidency, because it appealed to leftists. These people believed that the aristocracy should be stripped of its power. The movement hid underground during the Pinochet dictatorship, when leftists were viewed as enemies of the state. The present openness has resurrected New Song.

Viola Para (1917–1967) and Victor Jara (1934–1973) are the most famous New Song artists. They both died tragically. Viola Parra is the "mother" of the movement. She was a gifted singer, prolific composer, and brilliant songwriter. Tormented by personal problems, Parra committed suicide at age 50. In the late 1960s, American singer Joan Baez sang Para's best song—"*Gracias a la vida*" (I Give Thanks to Life)—at popular concert performances, making Para an international celebrity posthumously (after death).

Like Viola Para, Victor Jara composed and sang many songs that would become part of the New Song movement. In the days following the military coup in 1973 that gave rise to Pinochet's dictatorship, government troops rounded up thousands of supposed enemies of the state. The troops took them to Santiago's National Stadium for questioning. Jara was among the prisoners. Military interrogators tortured and killed hundreds of people at the stadium. The 29-year-old Jara was among them.

> Victor Jara of Chile
> Lived like a shooting star
> He fought for the people of Chile
> With his songs and his guitar
> His hands were gentle, his hands were strong
>
> —"Victor Jara." Lyrics by Adrian Mitchell, music by Arlo Guthrie (1990). Source: Lyrics Connection.

During the remainder of the 1970s and most of the 1980s, political and governmental deterioration led to the deaths of outspoken leftist leaders, like Victor Jara, and to other horrific acts. Since 1990, the country has undergone political reconciliation and now has a more stable government.

5

Government and Politics

C hile has a democratic government that allows every adult the right to vote. Its laws apply to everyone. Its citizens have the right to receive fair trials, and they can meet and discuss freely their political and religious beliefs. As a democratic government, the nation educates its citizens, which enables them to make informed decisions about political issues. Chileans' present freedom evolved through a series of constitutions.

The country has had three constitutions. The first two charters, the Constitutions of 1833 and 1891, created republican governments. Citizens of a republic elect politicians to represent them in government. These early governments, however, were by no means democratic. They only protected the rights and privileges of the wealthy aristocracy. What is more, only literate males could vote and run for office. In addition to women, this requirement excluded the majority of male members of early Chilean society.

The Constitution of 1925 was more democratic. The charter gave people from all levels of society the right to vote and participate in government. Initially, the document allowed only men who could read and write the right to vote, but amendments eventually opened voting booths and public service to women and illiterate people as well. The charter also modeled Chile's government after that of the United States. It was divided into three branches with checks and balances to ensure that a few individuals could not take control of the government. The Constitution of 1981 and later amendments gave rise to Chile's present government.

STABILITY OF EARLY REPUBLICAN GOVERNMENTS (1833–1925)

Although they were undemocratic, the Constitutions of 1833 and 1891 established the most durable governments in Latin America from 1833 to1925. The Chilean people followed the rule of constitutional law. Neither violence nor revolution forced a single Chilean president out of office during this period. Presidents took one another's place by electoral means. No other country in Latin America had such a lengthy record of stability. Most of them had governments similar to Chile's, but civil wars typically cut short presidencies after a few years.

Historians have long questioned why Chile's early governments did not give way to civil war like other Latin American governments did. Scholars point to several interrelated factors that prolonged the existence of Chile's governments. First, Chile's earliest area of settlement—middle Chile—had a homogeneous (of the same kind) Spanish and Spanish-mestizo population. Thus, racial tension and uprisings were not problems there. There was virtually no African population. The Mapuche Indians were thoroughly defeated and conveniently tucked away in reservations in the south (a policy that still blemishes the nation's reputation today).

The existence of settlement frontiers is a second reason Chile's early governments survived. As the nineteenth century wore on, slow settlement of the frontiers to the north and south from middle Chile took place. This outward migration provided a safety valve for middle Chile's growing population. There were certainly frustrations among the migrants, particularly because of poor labor practices in the mines where many of them found work. Two small mid-century revolts took place in the frontier as a result. All the same, rather than creating a serious challenge to the authority of middle Chile, the frontier, gave an overflow population a sense of opportunity and hope.

A third reason why Chile's constitutional government survived is that it did not have a hollow frontier. A hollow frontier is one in which active settlement occurs only on the edge of an expanding frontier. No solid network of towns develops between the edge and the main area of settlement. Such geographical isolation could lead to injustices, misunderstandings, regional rivalries, violent clashes, and civil wars. In Chile, roads, railroads, and ocean shipping lines connected the country's frontier areas to middle Chile, the core area of settlement. Such lines of communication between people at the periphery and the center helped keep the nation together.

A successful nineteenth-century economy is a fourth reason why Chile's early governments survived for so long. Chile's output of copper and silver increased during this period. The country was the world's leading copper exporter by 1860, a position it still holds today. Agricultural production also increased. A mid-century boom in wheat sales to California and Australia proved temporary. Rising exports to the British market made up for that loss. Until the 1890s, Chilean wheat production was still greater than that of Argentina, Chile's main South American rival producer. The government invested tax money (mainly from nitrate exports) to build the continent's first telegraph network. The government and foreign investors built railroads into the interior and established steamship lines along the coast. This network was for interregional

Chile has a democratic government that has evolved through a series of constitutions over the past two centuries. Here, in 2002, Chile's president addresses the National Congress in Santiago. The coat of arms, seen behind the president, features two national symbols of Chile, the Andean condor, and the huemul, a near extinct species of deer indigenous to the country.

trade, but it also helped unify the nation politically. Just as important, the booming economy created jobs for Chileans, so they were less likely to complain about the shortcomings of their government.

THE EARLY DEMOCRATIC PERIOD
(1925–1973)

Authors of the 1925 constitution modeled it after the U.S. Constitution. The charter divided the government into three equal branches: the executive, legislative, and judiciary. A house of deputies and a senate composed the legislative branch. After a few amendments, the constitutions gave all citizens of Chile the right to vote. The charter guaranteed other freedoms that true democracies have as well, such as the freedoms of assembly, religion, speech, and so on. The charter also gave the government the job of providing social security, including setting standards for public health, housing, and sanitation, and enforcing safety regulations in the workplace.

Conservative elements in Chile believed that government should not have such responsibilities. Shortly after the constitution took effect, there was a brief period of dictatorial rule under Colonel Carlos Ibáñez. After that, the nation went through a sustained period of electoral democracy. A more serious rebellion rocked Chile in 1973, when Augusto Pinochet took over the government.

THE FALL OF DEMOCRACY UNDER PINOCHET
(1973–1990)

In the late morning of September 11, 1973, army tanks and air force planes bombarded the *La Moneda*, Chile's presidential palace. There had been rumors for months about a possible military coup. The Marxist policies of President Salvador Allende had lost the support of key members of his political coalition. There was a serious food shortage and rampant inflation, rising unemployment, and illegal seizures of private property by labor and trade unions. Allende and a handful of his closest advisors and personal bodyguards had rushed to *La Moneda* earlier that morning to discuss reports of a possible military uprising. Allende gave a radio address pledging his

Democracy disappeared in Chile from 1973–1990 during the rule of dictator Augusto Pinochet. This photograph shows the Chilean Army firing on La Moneda Palace in Santiago under Pinochet's leadership during the 1973 coup. Pinochet held violent, absolute rule in Chile until 1990 when he agreed to step down after a special vote showed Chileans did not want him in office.

defense of his right to govern. A short time later, he was dead. Facing the certain end of his presidency, he chose to take his own life.

General Augusto Pinochet, born in Santiago and educated

in Chile's military academy, led the revolt. A military junta (a group of generals) ran the new government. Pinochet was its leader. During the 1970s, the junta suspended the constitution. It gave the military and national police force almost unlimited power. They arrested, detained, and jailed protesters without trials. Evidence indicates that Pinochet also directed a secret police force to track down former Allende supporters. This group tapped telephones, opened mail, and kidnapped suspects. Thousands of political prisoners were murdered, jailed, tortured, brutalized, or exiled. In an effort to completely silence critics, Pinochet and his military commanders closed congress, censored the media, purged the universities, burned books, outlawed political parties, and banned labor union activities. No one expected that the military regime would be so bloody and so long lasting, not even the coup's harshest critics.

By the early 1980s, Pinochet was confident that he was in control of the country. He eased up on his hold by allowing passage of a constitution in 1981. This constitution was rooted in the Constitution of 1925. Under Pinochet's watchful eye, authors of the Constitution of 1981 created a strong executive (president) but a weak congress and judiciary. For example, it allowed Pinochet (who was the president) to dissolve the chamber of deputies if he saw fit. The charter also gave the president power to pick one-third of the senators. Pinochet's control was absolute. People were afraid to voice their opinions in public or private, for fear of the secret police. Nonetheless, with unemployment at record levels and cutbacks in welfare programs being felt everywhere, Chileans became increasingly militant in demanding an immediate return to democracy.

Despite these rumblings, Pinochet was still very confident in his control of the country. In 1989, he held a plebiscite (special vote) calling for the people to vote "yes" or "no" on whether they wanted him in office. A "yes" vote would mean that Pinochet would remain as president until 1998. A "no" vote would mean that new, open elections would be held in late 1989. The "no" voters won. A surprised Pinochet agreed to quit at the end of 1989.

TODAY'S GOVERNMENT

Ironically, Pinochet's 1981 constitution is the basis of Chile's modern democratic government. Revisions in 1989, 1993, and 1997 transformed the constitution into a democratic document. Some experts see further constitutional reform as necessary to complete the changeover to democracy.

In its present form, Chile's constitution pledges the three branches of government equal power through a system of checks and balances. It allows people of all political parties, ethnic backgrounds, and religious persuasions to take part in government. It also allows the people to elect the president. The people elect members of the legislature and municipal governments as well. The charter promises the right to vote to all citizens and foreigners who have resided in the country for more than five years, if they are 18 years of age or older. (Women got the right to vote in 1934 for municipal elections and in 1949 for national elections.)

The executive branch includes the president and his cabinet. The president must be at least 40 years of age and born in the country. He or she is elected to a six-year term and cannot serve two consecutive terms. The president appoints a cabinet of ministers to direct various functions of government. The makeup of the cabinet includes ministers of foreign relations, agriculture, finance, health, defense, public works, mining, housing, and so on. There are 18 cabinet ministries and 4 cabinet-level agencies. The president also appoints members of the judiciary and other officials to govern the nation's territorial divisions. Furthermore, the president appoints members of the Supreme Court, as well as all appellate court and local court justices. These appointments are final and not subject to approval by congress.

Chile's constitution gives the legislative branch the power to select a new president with a majority vote if two years or less are left in the presidential term. Should the vacancy occur with more than two years left in the term, the legislature must call for a nationwide presidential election.

The constitution provides for a bicameral (having two houses) legislature consisting of a senate and chamber of deputies (the equivalent of the House of Representatives in the U.S. Congress). Congress has a 48-seat senate. Senate members must be citizens, at least 40 years old, have completed high school, and have lived in the region they represent for at least four years. They serve eight-year terms, with half the senate coming up for election every four years. People elect 38 of the 48 senators. Nine senators receive appointments from the Supreme Court, the National Security Council, and the president. Four of these appointees must be former commanders of the armed forces. There is one senator for life. (The constitution entitles former presidents to a lifetime senate seat.) The chamber of deputies consists of 120 members, 2 for each of 60 congressional districts. All deputies serve four-year terms. When their term begins, they must be citizens, at least 21 years old, have graduated from high school, and have lived in the district they represent for at least two years.

The hierarchy of Chile's court system has four levels of jurisdiction. Beginning at the top, they are the Supreme Court, appellate courts, major claims courts, and local courts. The Supreme Court consists of 17 members. The Court reviews appeals by defendants who lost cases in the lower, appellate courts. Unlike the U.S. Supreme Court, the Chile Supreme Court does not review Congress' laws in order to determine if they go against the constitution. A special Constitutional Tribunal is set up for that purpose.

Chile has 16 appellate courts, each with jurisdiction over one or more provinces. The majority of these courts have 4 presiding judges, although the two largest courts have 13 members, and Santiago's Appellate Court has 25. The appellate courts rule on laws that apply to the provinces within their jurisdictions and hear appeals by defendants who lost their cases in the major claims and lower courts.

GOVERNMENTAL TERRITORIES

Chile is organized into a hierarchy of territories. From largest to smallest, the hierarchy includes administrative divisions, provinces, and communes. Like vertebrae of a spinal column, 13 large administrative divisions divide the narrow country (Table 2). Except for Metropolitan Santiago, the divisions include a bit of West Coast, Central Valley (or Inland Waterway), and Andean crest. (Metropolitan Santiago does not reach the coast.) Chile's president appoints an *intendente* (subtreasurer) to run each division. For organizational purposes, the government uses roman numerals to identify 12 of the 13 divisions. The numerals run one after the other from north to south, beginning with Region I at the north end of the country, and finishing with Region XII at the southern end. Metropolitan Santiago, which includes Santiago and its suburbs, is the thirteenth division.

Region XII (Magallanes) is the largest of the 13 divisions. It includes Chilean Antarctica, a wedge-shaped slice of the Antarctic continent. Metropolitan Santiago is the smallest of the 13 divisions, but it is by far the most populous area. Region XI (Aisén) has the smallest population. The region consists of remote islands of the southern archipelago and a highly glaciated section of the Andes.

Table 2: Chile's Administrative Divisions and the Number of Provinces in Each Division*

REGION	NAME OF DIVISION	PROVINCES
I	Tarapacá	3
II	Antofagasta	3
III	Atacama	3
IV	Coquimbo	3
V	Valparaíso	7
	Metropolitan Santiago	6
VI	General B. O'Higgins	3
VII	Maule	4
VIII	Bío Bío	4
IX	Araucania	2
X	Los Lagos	5
XI	Aisén	4
XII	Magallanes	4

* The divisions are listed according to their locations in the country from north to south. This is why Metropolitan Santiago is listed in the table between Regions V and VI.

Provinces make up administrative divisions. There are 52 provinces. Table 2 shows the number of provinces in each division. In order to even out the number of people living in each province, the central government has varied the area and number of provinces in each division. For example, Region I (Tarapacá) has

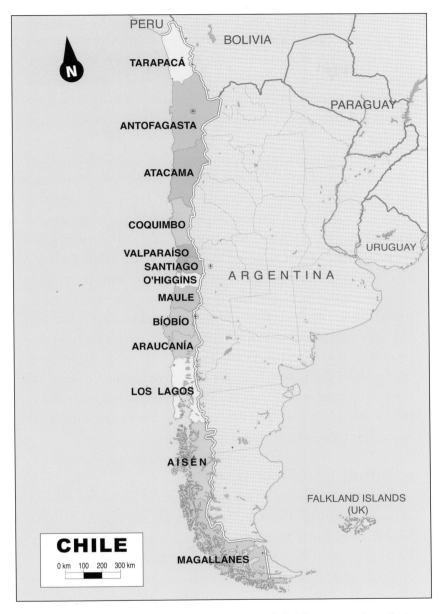

Chile is organized into thirteen governmental divisions or regions that run from north to south along the narrow country. Each division is separated into provinces, which are then divided into communes. This map shows the location and size of each division.

a small total population, but a major city—Arica. The remainder of the region is largely empty desert. As a result, the province that includes the city of Arica is smaller than the other two provinces. In contrast, Region V (Valparaíso) is a densely settled province with many towns and cities, including the city of Valparaíso. This region is broken down into seven provinces that are about equal in area.

Communes make up the provinces. They include both urban and rural areas. Communes handle the nuts and bolts of running local government. They deal with traffic regulation, land use planning and zoning, garbage collection, sewage, water supply, beautification, and so on. Each commune with an urban area has a council and a mayor who serve four-year terms. Citizens elect the commune council, which in turn appoints the mayor. The mayor picks delegates to run communes in remote rural areas. The mayor also proposes a budget and land use plans for the municipality. The council approves or rejects the mayor's proposals. It also approves local laws and rules and watches over the work of the mayor. The Chilean government provides an interesting Internet web page (in Spanish) with a map that shows the location of and data for all of the country's governmental territories (www.censo2002.cl).

NATIONAL BOUNDARY DISPUTES

Territorial boundaries are sometimes the subject of dispute between nations. The Chilean government has had three boundary disputes in recent years. Chileans and Argentines asked Pope John Paul II to settle a dispute over which country owned a cluster of three barren islands south of Tierra del Fuego. Although the islands themselves are insignificant, the country that owns them has fishing rights to a large area of the southern Atlantic Ocean. The pope's representatives concluded that the three islands belonged to Chile, and the two countries signed a treaty agreeing to the Pope's decision in 1985.

A second dispute involves Chile's northern border and is ongoing. Bolivia and Peru want to reclaim territory they lost to Chile in the War of the Pacific (1879–1884). Bolivia wants to reestablish the access it had to the Pacific Ocean before the war. Entry to the Pacific would require a corridor of land through northern Chile, but it would improve Bolivia's international trade. Chile would lose rights to minerals and water in the corridor. The dispute led to the cutoff of diplomatic ties between Chile and Bolivia in 1978. The two countries no longer operate embassies in the other's capital. They do maintain consulate offices, however, so that they can issue visas and passports to citizens of the other country. In 1979, on the one-hundredth anniversary of the start of the war, Peru's military signaled that it might try to retake the land it had lost in the war. Chileans primed for war, but the threat never materialized. Chile and Peru still have formal, although strained, diplomatic ties.

A third boundary dispute involves Chile's claim to a wedge-shaped section of Antarctica. The meeting of 53° and 90° west longitudes at the South Pole defines the wedge. In 2002, 130 Chileans, mostly scientists and their staffs, lived in Chilean Antarctica. Great Britain and Argentina claim areas that overlap Chile's claim. This dispute is not a pressing concern, because territorial claims to this continent are on hold by international agreement.

FOREIGN RELATIONS

Chile is a founding member of the United Nations. The country has been taking on key roles in the UN since its return to democracy in 1990. It served a two-year term on the United Nations Security Council in 1996–1997 and began a second two-year term in January 2003. It is also a member of the United Nations Commission on Human Rights. In recent years, Chileans have served as UN peacekeepers in Cyprus, Palestine, Pakistan, and India.

The country is also active in Latin American and other regional summits. Such meetings bring together diplomats from many countries. The envoys discuss problems and concerns that their countries have in common. Chile hosted the second Summit of the Americas in 1998. It presided over the Rio Group (an organization of 19 Latin American and Caribbean countries) in 2001. The country is also a member of the Organization of American States (OAS). Chile was a key supporter of the common defense provisions of the OAS following the September 11, 2001 terrorist attacks on the United States. The country held the fifth conference of the Ministers of Defense of the Americas in 2002. It is also a member of the Asia-Pacific Economic Cooperation (APEC) forum.

Chile is also seeking trade with other countries. It joined the APEC forum in an effort to boost commercial ties to Asian markets. It has also entered into Free Trade Agreements (FTAs), which stimulate trade by reducing or eliminating tariffs (taxes on imports and exports) between trading partners. Chile has FTAs with Canada, Costa Rica, Ecuador, the European Union, Mexico, South Korea, and Venezuela. It also has a FTA with the European Free Trade Association (Iceland, Liechtenstein, Norway, and Switzerland). Chile signed an FTA with the United States, its main trading partner, in June 2003. Chile is also an associate member of Mercosur, which includes Argentina, Brazil, Paraguay and Uruguay, as are Bolivia and Peru. Membership in Mercosur allows Chile special trading access to neighbors.

RECENT NATIONAL POLITICS (1990–PRESENT)

After Pinochet stepped down, Chile's congress amended the 1981 constitution to return the nation to democracy. The country has had freely elected presidents since then. A constitutional amendment in 1993 made presidential terms six-year terms and nonconsecutive.

The major parties include the Christian Democrat Party, the National Renewal Party, the Party for Democracy, the Socialist Party, the Independent Democratic Union, and the Radical Social Democratic Party. The Communist Party (champion of the Marxist-Leninist philosophy) has not won a congressional seat in the last four elections. Chileans' politics involve a lot of coalition building, because there are so many political parties. In the 2001 congressional elections, the conservative Independent Democratic Union surpassed the Christian Democrats for the first time to become the largest party in the lower house.

Political ideologies divided government in the past but are less of a problem today. For example, politicians no longer give serious thought to the radical change that a one-party communist system would require. Chileans agree that democracy is working. As a result, they have turned their energies away from ideology and toward concrete issues such as growing their nation's economy.

6

Economy

C hile has one the world's best performing economies. A measure of a country's economic performance is the Gross Domestic Product (GDP). The GDP is the value of all goods and services produced by a country. From 1990 to 2000, Chile's GDP grew 5.2 percent annually. This was the highest rate of GDP growth among all Latin American countries and one of the highest rates in the world.

Chile depends heavily on exports to make its economy grow. Mining makes up more than 40 percent of the total value of exports. The country's main mineral exports are copper ores and refined copper (20 percent of total exports). Other exports include industrial products, fruits and vegetables, paper and paper products, and chemical and petroleum products. The main importers of Chilean products are the United States, Japan, the United Kingdom, and Brazil. Chile's imports are lower in value than its exports, resulting in a positive trade balance. The main imports are mechanical and electrical equipment, mineral products, chemicals, textiles, transport equipment, metal and metal goods, synthetic plastic, and rubber. The United States is the principal exporter to Chile, followed by Argentina, Brazil, China, and Japan.

FREE TRADE AND THE GLOBAL ECONOMY

Foreign business investments fuel Chile's exports and economic growth. The nation attracts foreign investment because of its free trade policy. Chile's policy does away with barriers to trade. The policy eliminates nearly all taxes on goods of foreign countries entering or leaving the country. In 2003, Chile was the only country in Latin America that qualified as having a barrier-free economy, according to a study by the Heritage Foundation and *The Wall Street Journal*. In fact, only 16 of 165 countries worldwide had a free economy that year. (The United States was one.)

Because of Chile's free trade policy, foreign companies have invested large sums of money and capital in the country. These investments have created businesses, jobs, and income for Chileans. In the 1980s and 1990s, foreign investors focused on putting money in copper mining. By the early twenty-first century, investors had shifted their focus. They were buying and operating seaports and communication, gas, water, and electrical utilities. U.S. companies are the primary investors. Other companies are from Italy, Spain, Australia, and the United Kingdom. Direct foreign investments made up 50 percent of Chile's GDP in 2002.

Free trade among nations was the basis for an unprecedented expansion of the global economy in the 1990s. Few people know that the small nation of Chile helped ignite the expansion. In the mid-1980s, a handful of economists from the University of Chicago and the Chilean government put the world's first national free-trade policy in place. Many other countries, including the United States, promptly followed Chile's example. The movement toward free trade quickly snowballed to spur on the global economy.

Chile has one of the best-performing economies in South America and even the world. Because of its free trade policy, Chile attracts foreign business investments as well as considerable trade. The busy harbor of Valparaíso, seen here, is the second busiest seaport in Chile and handles much of its imports.

In addition to its free trade policy, Chile appeals to foreign investors because it has a diverse economy in which to invest money. Expressions of that diversity are the country's distinct economic regions—the north, south, and middle. Each of these regions contributes to Chile's export-based economy.

Northern Chile

Mining and parched desert stamp a unity on this important economic region. Northern Chile corresponds to the administrative divisions of Tarapacá, Antofagasta, Atacama, and Coquimbo (or Regions I–IV, respectively). The collapse of the nitrate market at the end of World War I caused the sudden abandonment of mining towns in the region. Ghost towns from this collapse still dot northern Chile today. The surviving nitrate mines are in the Central Valley, between the latitudes of Iquique and Antofagasta. The main town is María Elena (population 12,400). The nitrates are part of the hard, salty crust that occurs in the Atacama Desert's dry lakebeds. A water pumping process dissolves the salts and places them into evaporation ponds. The scorching desert sun evaporates the water, leaving nitrate salt concentrations behind. The present mines supply sodium and potassium nitrates for making natural fertilizers. Iodine, lithium, boron, and magnesium are commercial by-products of the refining process. Chile is the world's leading producer of nitrates and lithium and the second largest producer of iodine (Bolivia is first). The north has about 75 percent of the world's nitrate reserves.

Copper is by far northern Chile's (and the nation's) most valuable export. The copper ore is near the earth's surface. The ore is in rocks along north-south geological fault lines. These faults align along the edge of the Andes Mountains. The mines also produce some silver, gold, and molybdenum, because the same geologic environment forms these minerals. Seven of the 10 largest copper mines in the world are in Chile; 5 of the 10 are in northern Chile (Table 3). Chile produces about one-third of the world's copper. The country has about 27 percent of the world's total reserves of copper ore.

Table 3: Top Ten Copper Mines in Tonnage (Metric Tons, 1999)

RANK	NAME	LOCATION	TONNAGE
1.	Escondida	Chile (Antofagasta Division)	959
2.	Grasberg	Indonesia (West Papua)	770
3.	Chuquicamata	Chile (Antofagasta Division)	620
4.	Morenci	United States (Arizona)	470
5.	Collahausi	Chile (Iquique Division)	410
6.	El Teniente	Chile (General Bernardo O'Higgins)	350
7.	Bingham Canyon	United States (Utah)	295
8.	Andina	Chile (Valparaíso Division)	250
9.	Candelaria	Chile (Copiapó Division)	220
10.	El Abra	Chile (Antofagasta Division)	210

Source: Government of Chile, Ministry of Mining.

An international consortium (Australia, the United Kingdom, and Japan) operates the Escondida mine, the world's largest open-pit copper mine. The mine has been operating since 1990. The wide-open pit, which is made by gigantic digging and earth-moving equipment, accounts for 8 percent of the world's total production of copper and 22 percent of Chile's total production. Codelco, the government's largest state-owned mining company, operates the Chuquicamata mine. It is the world's third largest copper mine (the Grasberg mine in Indonesia is the second largest).

Since the early 1990s, direct investments by foreign companies have upgraded the copper smelting technology. (Smelting is the process of crushing and then melting a metal ore to

Northern Chile is known for mining, and copper is the nation's most valuable export, with Chile producing one-third of the world's copper. The copper mine in this photograph is Chuquicamata, owned by the Chilean Copper Company.

remove nonmetal impurities.) The newer mining operations save money by exporting copper as concentrate (crushed ore from which most of the impurities have been removed). The exporting of concentrate begins by adding water to the concentrate to make soupy mudlike slurry (a watery mixture of insoluble matter). A pump at the mine then moves the slurry from the mine to a coastal port through a nine-inch pipeline. Facilities at the seaport dewater the slurry and transfer it to ships for export. The country that imports the copper concentrate finishes the refining process by melting the concentrate into copper slabs.

Northern Chile's coastal ports supply goods and services to mining towns in the interior. As ports, they are outlets for the region's copper, nitrates, and refined by-products. Tocopilla (population 32,200), because of its location near principal nitrate plants, and Charñal (population 15,000), as the outlet for large inland copper mines, are important exporting ports. The nitrate industry also creates jobs in the coastal ports of Antofagasta (population 267,000) and Iquique (population 198,000). These ports are important fishing and regional supply centers, because they are also endpoints of the road and rail routes across Chile into Bolivia and Argentina. Arica is another large city of the region. It is the end of the only railroad link between Bolivia and the Pacific Ocean. This city has also taken on significance as a winter beach resort in recent years.

The nutrient-rich waters of the Humboldt Current are the basis for a large fishing industry. Chile ranks third in the world in fish catch (China and Peru are first and second, respectively). Northern Chile contributes a great deal to this ranking. The catch includes anchovies, jack mackerel, and pilchard. Iquique is one of the world's principal ports because of its huge fishmeal exports. Fishmeal is ground-up dried fish. Anchovies, in particular, make up this product. Fishmeal is high in protein and therefore an excellent livestock food supplement. Fish oil, a by-product of fishmeal production, is an additive for the manufacture of many items, ranging from margarines to inedible varnishes and waterproofing agents.

The largest inland desert city is Calama (population 148,000). The Loa River emerges from the Andes and provides a basis for modest agriculture there. Grapes are the main commercial crop. The town's economy is also dependent on serving tourists and the workers from the nearby Chuquicamata mine. A tourist guidebook states that most of the staggering wealth produced at the mine "is absorbed by the rest of the country, but enough of it remains to give this desolate outpost in the wilderness a chance to entertain itself." Tourists stay overnight in Calama to visit the mine or to use the town as a base for excursions into the Andes.

Mining, agriculture, and pastoralism (raising livestock) form a trio of economic activity in the southern fringe of northern Chile. *El Norte Chico* (the Little North), as Chileans prefer to call this area, corresponds more or less with the Coquimbo administrative division (Region IV). Bethlehem Steel, a U.S. company, ran the world's largest iron mine between 1914 and 1954 at El Tofo. The company extracted the ore and shipped it from the Chilean port of Huasco to the Bethlehem Steel refinery and plant at Sparrows Point, Maryland. *El Norte Chico* has three iron ore mines now. An iron ore pellet plant at Huasco (population 8,100) supplies both domestic and foreign markets.

Small streams provide a basis for agriculture in the semiarid *El Norte Chico*. Small-scale irrigation for subsistence agriculture is the traditional economic activity in this semiarid land. The Copiapó, Limarí, and Elqui valleys are famous for making *pisco*, a potent grape brandy that is popular among Chileans. Dried peaches, raisins, and figs are also national favorites. In recent years, vineyards for table grapes have become more widespread, the result of irrigation projects funded by outside investors. These vineyards are for the international market. Each summer, the area's table grapes are the first in Chile to ripen and the first to hit U.S. supermarkets, usually around Christmas.

El Norte Chico's rainfall is low in amount, but it is enough to support scattered grasses and livestock ranching. Government efforts to break up large *haciendas* (livestock ranches) in this region have not been as effective as in middle Chile, so the landholdings are relatively large. The climate is too dry and the soil too poor to divide the land into smaller ownership parcels. La Serena (population 149,600) and Coquimbo (population 160,000) are the principal towns of this transition zone. The town of La Serena is an agricultural service center and a popular tourist resort. Coquimbo is a seaport with a relatively good harbor. Waterpower from the Limarí River is the basis for small industries in both towns.

Middle Chile

A Mediterranean climate, urban industry, and a rich agricultural economy stamp a unity on middle Chile. The region is made of the administrative divisions of Valparaíso, General Bernardo O'Higgins, Maule, and Bío Bío (Regions V–VIII, respectively), as well as Metropolitan Santiago. The area is the nation's smallest economic region, but it is Chile's most populous and wealthy region. The northern boundary is the Aconcagua River, and the southern limit is the Bío Bío River. Between these two rivers is a colorful mixture of agriculture, cities, and mining.

Middle Chile has more than 50 percent of the country's total agricultural landholdings. Grains occupy more than half the cropland. Wheat has been the most important grain crop there since colonial times. Fruit occupies much of the remaining land. Largely because of middle Chile's diverse production, Chile leads the Southern Hemisphere in fruit exports. Vineyards for table grapes and for making wine take up more land than any other fruit crop. Orchards of apples and avocados are also extensive in hilly sections of the region. Other fruits include lemons, oranges, nectarines, kiwifruits, cherries, raspberries, and strawberries.

The livestock industry is important to the economy as well. Land reforms have broken up most of the large haciendas, but there are still numerous smaller livestock-raising businesses. These operations use much of their land to raise animal feed. The ranchers feed the animals (cattle, sheep, and hogs) home-grown oats, barely, and corn. Towns nearby are service centers for the industry. They process livestock products, including leather goods (such as hats, shoes, and belts), woolen textiles, and meat products.

Metropolitan Santiago dominates the urban landscape. With a population of about 6.5 million people in 2003, the metropolis sprawls out over what used to be productive farmland. A main north-south corridor of road and rail lines connects Santiago to other industrial cities and market towns in the valley. Secondary lines, running east and west from the corridor, connect coastal and Andean foothill settlements. As in most urban hierarchies, the bulk of the people, goods, services, and money that enter this transportation network end up going to the largest urban center, Metropolitan Santiago.

Metropolitan Santiago's economy is so powerful that it dominates the entire nation. The metropolis employs about 40 percent of all the workers in the country. People find work in tourism, restaurants, hotels, department stores, and so on. They also find work in governmental, educational, and financial institutions. Many industries employ people to process farm and livestock products. Manufacturing is also a major source of jobs. Each year, Metropolitan Santiago's robust economy produces 40 to 45 percent of the nation's manufactured goods.

Four additional cities also contribute a great deal to middle Chile's urban economy. They are Valparaíso, Viña del Mar, Concepción, and Talcahuano. Valparaíso (population 296,000) is Santiago's main seaport. This city has an attractive coastal setting and draws thousands of tourists each year. Visitors come to enjoy the city's vistas, fresh seafood, and cafés. The city also draws visitors for its theaters, parks, colonial buildings, and museums. This city is the nation's second busiest seaport, with extensive dock facilities to handle the bulk of the country's imports. Most of the imports go directly to Metropolitan Santiago. Valparaíso also manufactures chemicals, textiles, paint, leather goods, clothing, metal products, vegetable oils, and sugar. In recent years, the port of San Antonia, 30 miles (50 kilometers) south of Valparaíso, has been handling more cargo than any other port in Chile.

Viña del Mar (population 328,000) is Valparaíso's northern neighbor. The city started in the nineteenth century as a resort haven for Valparaíso's growing middle class. Today, Viña del Mar's stylish hotels, glitzy nightclubs, and first-class restaurants make it a vacation spot for Chile's affluent upper class and foreign tourists. Many wealthy Chileans and other Latin Americans own second houses there. Even the president of Chile sometimes stays in Viña del Mar in a government-owned holiday villa. The city generates income from some industrial development, as well as from tourism and recreation.

The city of Concepción (population 222,000) is the center of economic activity on the southern fringe of middle Chile. A favorable location near the mouth of the Bío Bío River permits the city easy access to the interior. An excellent harbor in Talcahuano (population 297,000) is nearby. As a result, Concepción processes agricultural items (such as fruits) and forestry products (lumber and pulp, for example) from the Bío Bío valley and then exports the goods (such as jams, wood furniture, and paper products) through Talcahuano. Like Iquique in the north, the port of Talcahuano is an important exporter of fishmeal.

Concepción also benefits from Chile's only steel mill, which is at nearby Huachipato. The mill is an integrated plant, meaning all raw materials—iron ore, coke (is coal from which most gases have been removed by heating), and limestone—are brought to one location to produce rolled steel. Iron ore pellets come from Huasco. Furnaces burn coke to provide the heat necessary to melt the ore. Mill operators make coke by importing small amounts of high-grade coal from local mines. Limestone comes from rock quarries on Guarello Island, which is in the Chilean archipelago. Limestone is added to melted ore to remove impurities. Industries in the city of Concepción use Huachipato's rolled steel to fabricate a wide range of products.

Middle Chile's Bío Bío subregion is the nation's second largest coal-producing area (Magallanes in the far south is the largest). About two-thirds of the Bío Bío production comes from the Lota mines just south of Concepción. Farther south, on the Lebu Peninsula, is an area of low-grade coal that extends under the sea. Another coalfield is in the Chiloé area. In addition to coal mines, middle Chile has seven Andean copper mines, two of them—the El Teniente and Andina mines—are among the world's top ten producers (Table 3). El Teniente is also the world's largest underground mine. The mine has been operating since 1905. It includes more than 1,250 miles (2,000 kilometers) of tunnels, although only 500 miles (800 kilometers) yield ore today. The copper ore is shipped out of the country through the port of San Antonio.

Southern Chile

A rainy climate and forestry, dairies, and fishing stamp a unity on southern Chile. This economic region begins at the Bío Bío River and ends at the arrow-point tip of Tierra del Fuego. Integrating the region into the nation's economy took more than a century of slow immigration by Chileans and Europeans. Even today, parts of the region are so isolated that they are without electricity or telephones. Three subregions compose southern Chile's economic landscape: North End, Aisén, and Far South.

The North End

Araucania and The Lakes administrative divisions (Regions IX and X) make up the North End. The transport pattern is similar to that of Mediterranean Chile. A medial (north-south) trunk links the main market towns of the Central Valley. Angol (population 56,000), Temuco (population 259,000), Valdivia (population 140,000), and Osorno (population 150,000) are on the route. Side roads link the coast and Andean foothills to the valley. The North End's central trunk ends in Puerto Montt (population 168,000). The port city is also the connecting point for travelers going north to Santiago and south to the remainder of southern Chile.

Virtually all the North End cities are small industrial centers. Their industries include flour mills, breweries, tanneries, and woodworking plants, based principally on local raw materials. Throughout the region, tourism is becoming an important source of income. The basis of tourism is the area's interesting mix of German, Mapuche Indian, and mestizo cultures. The area's scenic countryside and recreational activities also attract many visitors.

Forestry is the most important economic activity of the North End. Private companies have ownership of vast tracts of forest-covered land. Their sawmills dot the landscape. Timber-laden trucks deliver logs to the sawmills. Farmers also cut trees for fuel and to be sold to sawmills. Band saws in the mills cut straight-trunk logs of fir and araucaria pine into narrow slabs of quality lumber. Chile's forestry industry also specializes in making wood pulp from chips. Each mill has a wood chipper that makes chips from low-grade wood. Pulp mills turn the chips into an oatmeal-like pulp. The mills turn the pulp into paper, cardboard, and particleboard products. The chemical industry also uses the pulp.

To conserve natural forest areas, the pulp industry depends heavily on fast growing, commercially planted trees, such as eucalyptus (from Australia) and *radiata* pine (from Austria).

About half of Chile's pulp production comes from such trees. Puerto Montt and Chiloé Island are the main pulp and lumber centers. Wood chips, pulp, lumber, and other wood products are the North End's most valuable exports. Japan, the United States, and Germany import most of these products.

The North End's agriculture takes place in areas where forests once stood. Unlike farmers in middle Chile, who export many of their crops to foreign countries, farmers in southern Chile sell most of their products to the domestic market. A common sight is dairy cows, beef cattle, and sheep grazing on the North End's lush pastures. This pastoralism is the basis for a growing dairy and meatpacking industry. The main market for this southern subregion's dairy and meat products is Metropolitan Santiago.

Many of southern Chile's North End crops are typical of temperate regions: apples, cherries, raspberries, and blueberries. Considerable quantities of sugar beets, potatoes, beans, and peas are also grown. A small linen industry depends on flax cultivation. The main commercial crop is wheat. The region's mild temperatures and relatively dry summer allow this crop to thrive in Araucania. In the Lakes Region, the climate is too wet and cool for wheat production. Ocean fishing and pulp production replace wheat as an important income sources there.

Aisén

Aisén is Chile's eleventh administrative division (Region XI). Most of this subregion of southern Chile consists of thousands of small islands, uninhabited save for a few hundred Alacaluf Indians. On the mainland, steep Andean slopes and water-filled valleys make the soil poor or nonexistent. Beyond the Andean crest are small areas of Chilean Patagonia, with its semiarid treeless plains and small streams.

Aisén is Chile's last resource frontier. Mining of copper, silver, lead, and zinc is in its infancy, as is harvesting the region's commercial timber and marine resources. The area remained isolated until the second half of the twentieth century. The only important town was Puerto Aisén. Hardy German immigrants had settled this lonely place, stuck at the end of an isolated fjord, in 1870. Puerto Aisén became the region's government and commercial center. Government officials rarely visited the outpost. Similarly, commerce was limited to an occasional supply ship plying the cold, fog-shrouded inland waterway between Puerto Aisén and Chiloé Island.

Aisén's mountains isolated the Chilean Patagonia even more. There were only a few struggling frontier cow towns there. Settlers from Argentina established these towns prior to 1940. These small communities were very much like those in the old west in the United States during the nineteenth century. Argentine cowboys (*gauchos*) tended to livestock. On days off, the gauchos often went wild in the towns. There was very little law enforcement, because the region was isolated from the seat of government in Puerto Aisén. There were a few rutted roads but none connected the towns to other parts of Chile. Virtually no products left Chilean Patagonia, aside from the scrawny cattle that gauchos herded to markets across the border in Argentina.

The frontier quality of Aisén began to change in 1976. In that year, the Chilean government began building the Southern Highway (*Carretera Austral*). The route today is mostly unpaved road with occasional ferry crossings. It starts at Puerto Montt and ends abruptly in southern Aisén, just beyond the small settlement of Cochrane. The road bypasses the government center of Puerto Aisén, although a branch joins the port to the highway.

The Southern Highway has changed Aisén. It has brought people into the region seeking jobs. Farmers are now selling crops—wheat, beans, rice, and fruit—to the growing local population. Livestock ranches and dairy farms are turning out commercial products in small amounts for national markets. Dairy and meatpacking plants also now operate in Puerto Aisén.

Many areas of southern Chile are isolated, and therefore in some regions, such as Aisén, mining and harvesting timber and marine resources are in their infancy. The chief source of income in this region is fishing; in fact, fishing is so successful here that Chile as a nation is second only to Norway in salmon exports. Here, salmon are processed by workers in a plant in the Pacific port of Chacabuco.

Because of its strategic location on the highway, Coyhaique (population 49,000) has surpassed Puerto Aisén (population 27,000) as the largest population center.

The chief income source of the Aisén subregion is fishing, with Puerto Aisén being the area's main fishing port. Chile is the second largest exporter of salmon after Norway, thanks largely to Aisén's contribution of caught, as well as farmed, salmon. Besides salmon, the fish catch includes trout, hake, king clip, and sea bass. Bottom-dwelling marine animals, including sea urchins, octopus, scallops, shrimp, and crabs, are also important commercial products.

In many ways, life in Aisén is not much different than it was before the Southern Highway came to the region. Many things that urban dwellers take for granted—doctors, schools, telephones, and newspapers—are still scarce. There are more cars and trucks now. Buses operate, but they often run late or not at all. The most common means of transportation is still horseback or wooden-wheeled carts drawn by oxen.

Far South

Southern Chile's far south sub-region corresponds with Magallanes, (Region XII). A north-south line joining the crests of the region's mountains divides the far south into two spheres. West of the line, Magallanes' mountains have some of the most rugged terrain in South America. Mercilessly torn apart by glaciers, the mountains' western edge forms the south end of Chile's archipelago. The surviving heights endure an endless pummeling by frigid rain and howling winds blowing in from the Pacific. The severe weather gnarls and stunts trees. Understandably, economic activity in the western half of Magallanes is absent, save for an occasional oil-drilling rig, fishing port, or mining operation.

The area east of the mountainous divide is of more economic use. Protected to some extent by the mountains, this plainlike area escapes enough of the Pacific Ocean's fury to have several towns. The settlements are centers of commerce, petroleum production, and fishing ports. More than 80 percent of the population resides in Punta Arenas (population 132,000). The area around Punta Arenas has been Chile's primary area of sheep grazing since about 1880. The far south has yielded important quantities of wool for export ever since.

Despite the historical importance of wool, petroleum (oil and natural gas) is the primary income source for this subregion. In 1945, oil and gas were discovered on the island of Tierra del Fuego. The Magallanes (named for Magellan, the explorer who passed through the strait in 1519) Strait separates

Punta Arenas from the island. Punta Arenas has become the center of a petrochemical industrial complex. The complex is the country's main domestic source of oil and natural gas. Tankers transport the oil to refineries in middle Chile. Natural gas is liquefied in plants on Tierra del Fuego and then shipped by tanker to supply cities in middle Chile. Plants on the Strait of Magellan produce chemical fertilizer and methanol for export as well. The country's largest coal deposits are at Peket, a few miles west of Punta Arenas. The coal is strip mined, meaning the overlying rock is removed to create a broad open-pit mine. A power plant at Tocopilla (in northern Chile) uses the entire output of this mine.

7

Living in
Chile Today

*We Chileans feel our bond with the soil, like the campesinos [rural folk]
we once were. Most of us dream of owning a piece of land, if for nothing
more than to plant a few worm-eaten heads of lettuce. Our most important newspaper, El Mercurio, publishes a weekly agricultural supplement
that informs the public in general of the latest insignificant pest found on
the potatoes or about the best forages for improving milk production. Its
readers, who are planted in asphalt and concrete, read it voraciously,
even though they have never seen a live cow.*
—ISABEL ALLENDE, *MY INVENTED COUNTRY* (2003)

URBAN LIVING

Nearly all Chileans live in cities. The typical Chilean city has
traditional-style, adobe buildings and quaint plazas in the
older sections. Modern-style offices and other buildings are

scattered along major streets. The tallest buildings hardly reach four or five stories in most cities. The suburbs range from hastily built *callampa* (mushroom in Chilean speech) settlements to fine modern homes that have well-kept flower and shrub gardens. Many of the callampa began as unplanned shantytowns, built by poor rural families moving to the city seeking jobs. The families could not afford high city rents, so they ended up living on the edge of the city. They built temporary homes from scrap lumber and cardboard. The government has made most of these settlements permanent by providing them with at least some public housing, mail service, schools, running water, and electricity. Yet many inhabitants of callampas are unskilled, undereducated, and unemployed.

Metropolitan Santiago has a much different feel than the country's other cityscapes, although it has its share of callampa settlements. A metropolitan area is a collection of growing cities. As decades pass, the cities grow together to form a nearly continuous carpet of homes, offices, factories, shopping malls, parking lots, and streets. This union has happened in Metropolitan Santiago. Most Chileans simply call the area Santiago, the name of the largest city and the nation's capital. Isabel Allende describes Santiago as a "demented octopus" that is "extending its tentacles in every direction."

As Santiago has grown, urban planners have built modern skyscrapers in the downtown center. The downtown is now a place of steel, glass, neon, and modern shopping malls and movie theaters. These same modern elements appear at major intersections along boulevards (Allende's octopus tentacles) that radiate from downtown. Like all large cities, Metropolitan Santiago has a fast-paced lifestyle. Three subway lines connect the downtown to sedate suburbs *(barrios)*.

Chile's urban society can be divided into three income groups: very rich, middle class, and poor. The very rich live in suburban mansions in the foothills of the Andes. The group includes the wealthiest 20 percent of the country's households. These families control about 40 percent of the nation's annual income. This is a big improvement since the 1950s, when 20 percent of the country's households controlled about 80 percent of the nation's annual income. Additionally, per capita income (the average income per person) has been rising since the 1990s. This trend has led to a rapid growth in the size of the middle class. The expanding economy has allowed more and more poor people to find better paying jobs. In 1987, people living in poverty made up 40 percent of the total population. By 1998, the poverty level had decreased to 22 percent.

Nevertheless, there is room for more improvement. Chile ranked a distant second behind Uruguay for the lowest poverty level in South America. (Uruguay's poor made up only 6 percent of the total population in 1998.) A nagging unemployment rate is too high, hovering between 9 and 10 percent during recent years. Most of the unemployed live in crowded shanty-towns, and the poorest of the poor still live in rural areas. Population geographers expect the rural poor to continue moving into cities with the hope of finding jobs. The inflow of people will continue to increase demands on an already strained urban environment.

LIVING WITH URBAN POLLUTION

Santiaguinos [residents of Metropolitan Santiago] have become accustomed to following the daily smog index just as faithfully as they keep track of the stock market or the soccer results.

—Isabel Allende, *My Invented Country* (2003)

The level of grime, noise, overcrowding, and traffic jams in Chile's cities is depressing. Metropolitan Santiago, which includes half of the nation's urban population, has one of the world's most serious air pollution problems. Each winter, cold, dense air from the Andes sinks into the city's valley. Warmer air aloft acts like a cap and traps pollutants in the cold air. With no place to go, Santiago's smoke, gasoline fumes, dust, and diesel soot build up in the cold air and turn it into a coppery haze (smog). As in the world's other cities that have major smog problems, there are days when the haze sickens and even kills babies in their cradles, old people in nursing homes, and birds in the air.

A big part of the air pollution problem is that Chileans drive too many cars. They drive more cars per populated land area than any other Latin American country (Table 4). In the struggle to stem air pollution, Chile's government requires that gasoline stations only pump lead-free fuel into cars. The government also requires that all Metropolitan Santiago vehicles built after 1992 must have catalytic converters that remove harmful pollutants from a car's exhaust and has set limits on gaseous emission from factories. The air is so awful that the city assigns days that vehicles can be driven based on their license plate number. A toll on cars entering the central city may be next, as more of the city's poor move into the middle class and behind the wheels of their own cars.

Table 4: Vehicles Per Populated Land Area in Latin America* (Top Ten Countries)

COUNTRY	VEHICLES PER SQUARE MILE	VEHICLES PER SQUARE KILOMETER
Chile	16.55	6.39
Venezuela	13.39	5.17
Argentina	12.10	4.67
Uruguay	11.40	4.40
Brazil	10.52	4.06
Ecuador	9.53	3.68
Colombia	8.88	3.43
Peru	3.68	1.42
Bolivia	2.12	0.82
Paraguay	2.02	0.78

*Based on averages for 1996–1999.
Source: World Bank data cited by Nationmaster.com
(www.nationmaster.com)

Metropolitan Santiago is not the only urban area with environmental woes. Water pollution is a widespread concern. The problem is most acute in shantytowns. Neighborhood councils ask people not to throw garbage or dump human waste into open drains and ditches, but people too poor to afford sewer connections have no choice. Large companies that are seeking to maximize profits are also guilty. The fishmeal industry is especially culpable. Rather than paying the expense of treating waste products, fish processing plants discharge entrails of fish into the ocean. Seawater is so polluted that authorities periodically have to close beaches near Talcahuano.

PLAZAS AND STREETS

The open-air plaza (town square), one of the basic elements of Chile's towns and cities, provides an escape from the pollution and daily turmoil of city life. The plaza is a transplant from Spain: Spanish colonists tried to recreate Spain's towns and cities in the New World. The Spaniards also included in their towns an orderly, rectangular grid of streets that enter plazas from all sides.

Plazas are beehives of social activity, because they are built in central locations. They are perfect places for townsfolk to meet and reminisce, gossip, discuss issues, or just to relax together. Private and public activities, such as parades, religious processions, weddings, speeches, and festivals, also take place in plazas. In the distant past, local authorities also used the plaza for public floggings and hangings.

Small towns have a single square plaza in their center. Large towns usually have one central or main plaza and several smaller or neighborhood plazas. Flower gardens and trees adorn most plazas. Typically, the squares have a water fountain or a statue of an important person who is associated with the town or nation. Spanish colonial law dictated that town plazas include a fort, church, jail, and *cabildo* (town hall). Each structure occupied a different side

Most Chileans live in urban areas, leading to serious pollution problems. Santiago has one of the worst air pollution problems, mostly because of the high number of cars in the city and surrounding metropolitan area. During the winter especially, Santiago is constantly capped by a thick layer of smog, as seen in this photograph.

of the square. Most plazas have undergone changes, but their basic function as a meeting place for people is still very important today. The most famous plaza in Chile is Plaza de Armas in Santiago's original center. Pedro de Valdivia originally laid out the town in 1541. The weapons (*armas*) he stored in the central plaza's fort are the basis of its name.

In the larger cities, there have been important changes in the classic Spanish street grid pattern. Diagonal, tree-lined boulevards interrupt the old right-angle pattern. City planners built these wide thoroughfares for rapid access to the city center from the suburbs. In Santiago, planners have also added subways to the classic pattern. Commercial activities that used to be prominent in plaza areas are now dispersed along the new routes. A hodgepodge of tall office buildings and modern apartments are replacing family homes along these routes.

FOOD AND FAMILY MEALS

If Marco Polo had descended on our coasts after thirty years of adventuring through Asia, the first thing he would have been told is that our *empanadas* are much more delicious than anything in the cuisine of the Celestial Empire [China].

—Isabel Allende, *My Invented Country* (2003)

Chileans prefer to eat traditional dishes (although many of these now come in frozen packages). The *empanada* is a popular turnover-type snack. It can be deep-fried or baked. It is made with a variety of fillings, including mince, chopped egg and olives, cheese, or even fruit. The empanada is popular in other parts of Latin America, but the onion-filled version is typically Chilean. The poor, who could not afford meat, originally ate it. *Humitas* and *pastel de choclo* are corn-based dishes. There are a variety of potato-based breads. Black beans cooked with corn and noodles are another popular dish.

Chile is not ideal vegetarian territory, because Chileans prefer to have meat as the main dish in a meal. The standard feast is a heart specialist's nightmare: a barbequed slab of beef topped with two fried eggs and buried in chips. The favorite restaurant among Chileans is the *parillada*. It specializes in a wide range of barbequed meat dishes. The most popular are

Open-air plazas are an important element of Chile's cities. They are built in central locations, and are a center of social activity as well as public activity such as parades, speeches, and festivals. Here, people play chess in one of Santiago's plazas.

beefsteaks, sausages, lamb chops, and pork chops. A topping of grilled udder parts and animal intestines is common. Seafood, which is more wholesome, is caught in the cold Antarctic and Humboldt currents and is the bases of popular dishes as well.

Before the early 1980s, the scent of fresh bread wafted through every neighborhood. The baker would hang a white cloth on a pole outside the door of the *panaderia* (bakery shop) to tell townspeople that the next batch of warm bread was out of the oven. Each day, the father of the family assigned someone the task of walking to the corner shop to buy the fresh bread. Trips to neighborhood markets for fresh meat, fish, and vegetables were also a part of the daily routine.

Now, nearly 90 percent of retail food sales take place in large shopping centers. Newer supermarkets often include bakeries, flower shops, extensive wine sections, and large dairy, meat, fish, and fresh produce departments. Meanwhile, new "hypermarkets" offer these products, as well as nonfood products and services. The larger food markets also stay open much longer than the neighborhood grocery store; some remain open nearly 24 hours, including weekends and holidays. Nevertheless, traditions seldom die away totally; in countless small towns, mom-and-pop grocery stores survive and white cloths still flutter in the breeze outside neighborhood panaderias.

Chilean families still try to eat meals together. Meals are seen as opportunities to share important moments with family and friends. Lunch and dinner can last from 45 minutes to two hours. Even so, like the decline in neighborhood panaderias, the tradition of the family having daily meals together is weakening.

There appear to be five factors behind this trend. First, fast-food franchises, which make it easier to have a quick meal, are multiplying. Second, more women are entering the workforce, so they have less time to prepare traditional meals. Third, there is a mounting acceptance of American foods, which makes fast foods more acceptable. Fourth, as cities grow, places of employment spread out spatially. Thus, family members who work are less able to come home in time for meals. Finally, most family members can fix their own meals, because frozen foods can be prepared in a microwave oven in a matter of minutes. Eating at home therefore does not require several family members be there to help prepare or cleanup after meals. The changing shopping patterns, attitudes, preferences, and technologies involving food are a reflection of the fast-pace of an urban, middle-class lifestyle. The changes are suggestive of the modern urban culture everywhere, for better or worse.

HEALTH AND EDUCATION

Chile also has modern health and educational facilities. Compared to citizens of other Latin American nations, Chileans have one of the highest life expectancies at birth, about 76 years. Chile's infant mortality rate is one of the lowest, at just over 9 deaths per 1,000 live births. These impressive numbers reflect Chile's excellent national heath care system. Access to the system is free of charge in case of indigents and those whose incomes fall below a certain level; 64 percent of Chileans receive help from the national heath care system. Virtually all remaining citizens have private health care insurance.

Except for the urban poor, most Chileans enjoy effective health care. Recent government programs have placed an emphasis on innovative programs. One program focuses on infant care and school lunches. An antismoking program concentrates on educating young people about the dangers of tobacco. The government also places high taxes on tobacco products to discourage smoking. In Chile, as in other industrialized nations, the major killers are cancer and heart disease; both diseases are related to tobacco usage. Deadly car accidents that are related to alcoholism are also of growing concern.

Most Chileans are interested in improving their mental and physical health. In recent years, exercise gyms have become popular among Chile's growing middle class. Chilean gyms follow the U.S. and European gym format, which offers a wide range of services. Exercise machines, professional instructors, swimming pools, saunas, spas, and even coffee bars for mental as well as physical relaxation are part of the offerings.

Chile's educational system is widely regarded as being one of Latin America's finest. Preschooling is open to children five years of age or younger. Basic education is compulsory for children ages 6 to 13. Secondary education lasts four years but is not compulsory. It includes students who are 13 to 17 years old. Adult education provides basic and secondary education for people who dropped out of regular schooling but wish to continue their education. The top universities include the University of Chile, the University of Concepción, the Catholic University of Chile, and the Catholic University of Valparaíso. Foreign educators recognize Chilean higher education as being among the best in Latin America. A few thousand Chileans study abroad, about one-fifth of them in the United States. The most popular careers among college graduates are teaching, medicine, engineering, and computer technology.

COMMUNICATIONS MEDIA

Chile is the most "wired" country in Latin America. The country has more Internet users (200 per 1,000 people in 2002) than any other Latin American country. (The United States has about three times as many users—591 per 1,000 people in 2002). Internet cafés are available, even in small towns, for those people who do not own a computer at home. The situation will improve because the government has recently reduced the cost of telephone service. In 2003, the government was in the process of providing high-speed connection services in Iquique, Antofagasta, Valparaíso, Concepción, and Santiago.

Like citizens in any modern democratic nation, Chileans have a wide range of newspapers, magazines, and electronic media to learn about what is happening at home and abroad. They are avid readers of newspapers, perhaps more so than people in the United States. There are about 30 national newspapers. The most read newspaper is *El Mercurio,* published in Santiago. The journalistic quality of this 50-page daily paper is comparable to the *Times* of London, the *New York Times,* or the *Chicago Tribune.* The large German-Chilean community reads the German-language publication *El Condor,* which is published once a week and is read regularly by 15,000 to 20,000 Chileans. The best source of Chilean news in the English language is the capital city's *Santiago Times.* All regional capitals have their own major newspapers.

Magazines are equally numerous. The most popular weekly news magazines are *Que Pasa* and *Ercilla.* They are similar to *Time* and *Newsweek,* in that they cover a wide range of national and international topics. *Casas* (Homes) is Chile's *Good Housekeeping* magazine. Its *Sports Illustrated* is *El Gráfico* (The Graphic).

Castillo-Feliâu (author of *Culture and Customs of Chile*) believes that *Condorito* (Little Condor) is the quintessential Chilean magazine. Newsstands have sold it since 1945. The main character is an Andean condor that "is to Chile what the bald eagle is to Mexico and the United States." Castillo-Feliâu describes Condorito as having human traits, "much like Walt Disney's Mickey Mouse, Donald Duck, and Goofy." Aside from his bird's head and beak, Condorito is human. He changes his character but never his Chilean personality; he can be "a bum, a salesman, a policeman, a physician—in short, he can assume any role or profession that exists in Chile." Castillo-Felix believed that the success of this magazine "lies in the way its creator can depict Chilean reality at an apparently comedic level, in much the same way the *All in the Family* and *I Love Lucy* did in the U.S. television from the 1950s though the 1970s." Yahoo, Inc. maintains a web page that describes, in Spanish, *Condorito's* group of characters. The site also provides recent excerpts from the magazine.

Chileans live in some very far-flung places, ranging from the windblown canyons in the north to icy coastal fjords in the south. Modern radio and television connect all but the country's poorest and most remote people to the outside world. The technology and service in Chile is virtually identical to that in the United States. The only difference is that their availability came a few years later in most cases. Radio dates back to the 1920s and television to 1959. There are 18 radio stations in the country. Programming includes Chilean folk music, classical music, and popular music, including foreign performers such as Madonna, Spice Girls, Bob Dylan, the Rolling Stones, the Beatles, and The Doors.

There are five television channels in Chile. Television entertainment took on a decidedly international flavor in 1986, when satellite transmission began. In addition to domestic channels, Chileans have cable, which gives them access to providers worldwide. Cable channels include CBS Telenoticias, TNT, HBO Ole, Discovery, Discovery Kids, Warner, Fox, ESPN, Sony Entertainment, MTV, Cartoon Network and others from the United States. Spanish is dubbed in nearly all TV (and cinema) movies; subtitles showing the original English script are rarely included. CNN is received in both English and Spanish. Other TV channels come in German, Italian, and other languages.

LEISURE AND SPORTS

Around the house, watching TV is the main leisure activity. *Telenovelas* (soap operas) produced in Chile, Mexico, Brazil, Argentina, and Columbia are popular. Seventy percent of Chileans follow the national soaps on a daily basis. Unfortunately, this kind of activity contributes to obesity. As they are doing in all modern countries, medical doctors in Chile are pointing to too much TV watching as a main cause of the problem. Health officials everywhere agree that solving the obesity problem requires regular exercise and healthy eating habits.

Fortunately, Chileans are not total "couch potatoes." Taking time off and visiting the countryside are important family traditions. Chile is a small country, so getaway locations are always nearby. The ocean's surge calls many families to the sea. Chile's excellent highways provide access to fashionable seaside resorts in less than two hours. Day-trippers and week-end vacationers arrive by private car or public bus. Popular resorts include Concon, Viña del Mar, San Antonio, Zapallar, and Cartagena. Body surfing, boogie boarding, surfboarding, windsurfing, sailing, and sea kayaking are popular activities. Equally as popular are trips to the north end region of southern

Chile to spend a day or two on a lakeside beach. Glacial lakes and nearby freshwater streams offer excellent trout fishing. The trout are sweet, plump, and delicious drawing anglers from all over the world.

Skiing is also popular among Chile's middle and wealthy classes. Ski resorts in the Andes stretch from just north of Santiago all the way to Patagonia. The most famous ski resort is Portillo. It is a short trip for many Chileans, because it is only about 90 miles (145 kilometers) east of Metropolitan Santiago. Besides Chilean urbanites, Portillo attracts skiers from countries in the Northern Hemisphere. Foreign skiers are able to begin their ski season early, because Portillo's season runs from the middle of June until the middle of October. In addition to skiing, the Andes offer hiking, camping, snowboarding, and mountain biking.

Chileans from all backgrounds enjoy watching horseracing, equestrian (horsemanship) competitions, and tennis. Soccer (*fútbol* in Spanish) is Chile's main spectator sport. Thousands of Chileans watch professional teams in large stadiums in the country's principal cities. Soccer is not just watched, however. Chileans play it with passion at all ages. Children often begin playing the game at a very young age, sometimes as soon as they are able to walk. It is common to see an entire Chilean family—preteens, teens, fathers, mothers, and even grandparents—enjoying a backyard soccer game on weekends or during holidays.

WEIGHTS AND MEASURES, TIME, AND HOLIDAYS

Chile uses the metric, rather than English, system of weights and measures. Grams and kilograms, not ounces and pounds, appear on packages. Meters and kilometers, not feet and miles, designate distances. Hectares, not acres, reference areas.

Chile is four hours behind Greenwich Mean Time (or universal time coordinates). If it is 3:00 P.M. in Santiago,

Sports are an integral part of Chilean life, and soccer is the country's most popular sport. Thousands of Chileans watch soccer and also passionately play it, starting at a young age. Members of the teams from Universidad Catolica and Colo Colo are pictured fighting for the ball in a 2002 championship game at the National Stadium in Santiago.

it will be 7:00 P.M. in Greenwich, England. The country does not observe daylight savings time. In other words, Chileans do not turn their clocks ahead an hour in the spring ("spring forward") and back an hour in the fall ("fall back") in order to have an extra hour of daylight during the summer.

Chileans observe several public holidays when most shops, offices, and museums close. They take time off to celebrate New Year's Day along with the rest of the world on January 1.

They observe Good Friday and Easter in March or April, but the exact dates vary. Other public holidays are Labor Day (May 1) and Naval Victory Day (May 21), which commemorates a naval battle between Chile and Peru during the War of the Pacific. Additional national holidays are Saint Peter and Saint Paul's Day (June 29), Assumption of the Virgin (August 15), National Independence Day (September 18), Armed Forces Day (September 19), All Saints' Day (November 1), Immaculate Conception Day (December 8), and Christmas Day (December 25).

8

Chile
Looks Ahead

Nighttime.
Among the islands
our ocean throbs with fish,
touches the feet, the thighs,
the chalk ribs
of my country.
The whole night
clings to its shores, by dawn
it wakes up singing
as if it had excited a guitar.
—PABLO NERUDA, EXCERPT FROM
THE POEM TITLED "ODE TO THE BOOK"

Pablo Neruda, Chile's national poet, wrote this poem to express his belief in the spiritual strength of the Chilean people. The nighttime is the darkness of Chile's uncertain future. The guitar is the land. The Chilean people are the dawn; they have the power and energy to strum the guitar, awaken the darkness, and reveal the future in song. The Chilean people should achieve great success, if they take advantage of their nation's fortunate physical geography, history, and culture.

We have explored how Chile has a fortunate physical geography. The country's long expanse has a diverse climate and natural resource base. During Chile's history, natural barriers have protected the country—the vast Pacific Ocean on the west, the towering Andes to the east, the world's driest desert in the north, and a cold and inhospitable land to the south. Insulated from the outside world, middle Chile became the nation's populous center and democratic heartland.

As the nation grew, a trade and communication system united outlying regions with the heartland. Serious regional disagreements and armed conflicts did not develop, so middle Chile remained the only power base. As a result, Chileans worked out their differences with less violence than did their South American neighbors. Chilean presidents, with a few exceptions, took one another's place by electoral means. As the power of Chile's aristocracy lessened, the country's government became even more democratic. The whole time, people of diverse backgrounds blended into a homogenous "melting pot" of Chilean culture.

As the twenty-first century begins, the country's location on the edge of an open sea and its land resources sustain an economy based largely on foreign trade. The world's other nations envy this out-of-the-way country. Chile has a rich land, a stable democracy, an attractive culture, and is an economic success.

Chileans are brimming with self-confidence, so much so that Chile's newspapers refer to Chile as "The new Argentina," South

Though Chile faces many challenges in the future, its rich land, stable economy, strong democracy, and unique culture will help the nation find success in the coming years. The children of Chile, like those enjoying the traditional celebrations for the Virgin del Carmen in this photograph, can hopefully look forward to growing up in a spirited country of prosperity.

America's other economic success story. Argentina, however, has fallen on hard times in recent years, and Chile knows that like its neighbor, it faces many future challenges. A trading nation, Chile is far too dependent on copper exports, which account for 20 percent of the country's revenue. As the price of copper goes up or down, so does the nation's economy. Chile is diversifying its trade to include more manufactured and value-added products in order to stabilize its future economy. It has also opened up free-trade agreements with many countries in hope of expanding its range of export items.

Chile faces other challenges as well. Air pollution is a serious problem. Automobile exhaust and choking smog obscure the magnificent view of the Andes on Santiago's eastern skyline. Freeway congestion and commuting times are increasing. A high rate of unemployment persists, as does the gap between the rich and poor. Shantytowns need more schools and health clinics. Demands on soil, forest, and ocean resources are increasing. Wildlife species are disappearing, and water pollution is also a growing concern. Modernization is changing the quality of people's lives. Many Chileans are nostalgic for the time when the television did not dominate family leisure and are unhappy trying to juggle demands of jobs and family. There is also anger and a nagging pain over the long trail of blood and suffering left by the Pinochet regime. The Chilean nation must deal with these issues in the coming years.

Chile has the tools necessary to meet many of these challenges. The country is politically stable; it has relied on the democratic process to remove a dictator and to elect its presidents since democracy was restored. This nonviolent transition of governments shows that Chileans are committed to never allowing a reoccurrence of misdeeds and injustices like those of the Pinochet regime. There are other reasons for optimism: Chile has one of the highest literacy rates in world, the educational and health care systems are among the best in South America, and the government has made sound economic policy decisions.

What are Chile's prospects for the future? As Neruda says, only the will of the Chilean people can strum the guitar and turn the darkness of the future into spirited song. Nonetheless, judging from Chile's land resources, democratic past, and present policies, the world can expect an exhilarating and prosperous performance!

Fact at a Glance

Total Area	292,260 square miles (756,950 square kilometers)
Climate	Temperate; desert in north; Mediterranean in central region; cool and damp in south
Terrain	Low coastal mountains; fertile central valley; rugged Andes in east
Highest Point	Nevado Ojos del Salado, 22,566 feet (6,880 meters)
Natural Resources	Copper, timber, iron ore, nitrates, precious metals, molybdenum, hydropower
Land Use	Arable land (2.65%); permanent crops (0.42%); other (96.93%)
Irrigated Land	7,000 square miles (18,000 square kilometers)
Natural Hazards	Severe earthquakes; active volcanism; avalanches; tsunamis
Population	15,700,000 (July 2003 estimate)
Population Growth Rate	1.06 (2003 estimate)
Net Migration Rate	0 migrant(s)/1,000 population (2003 estimate)
Life Expectancy at Birth	76.35 years (2003 estimate)
Ethnic Groups	white and white-Amerindian, 95%; Amerindian, 3%; other, 2%
Religions	Roman Catholic, 89%; Protestant, 11%; Jewish and other, negligible
Language	Spanish
Literacy	95.2% (age 15 and over can read and write)
Government Type	Republic
Capital	Santiago
Administrative Divisions	13 regions: Aisén, Antofagasta, Araucania, Atacama, Bío Bío, Coquimbo, General Bernardo O'Higgins, Los Lagos, Magallanes and Chilean Antarctica, Maule, Metropolitan Region (Santiago), Tarapacá, Valparaíso.

Note: The United States does not recognize claims to Antarctica.

GDP	$153 billion (2002 estimate)
Labor Force by Occupation	Agriculture, 11%; industry, 34%; services, 55% (2003 estimate)
Industries	Copper, other minerals, foodstuffs, fish processing, iron and steel, wood and wood products, transport equipment, cement, textiles
Agricultural Products	Wheat, corn, grapes, beans, sugar beets, potatoes, fruit; beef, poultry, wool; fish; timber
Export Commodities	Copper, fruits, paper and pulp, chemicals
Exports – Main Partners	United States, 17%; Japan, 14%; United Kingdom, 6%; Brazil, 5%; China, 5% (2000)
Import Commodities	Consumer goods, chemicals, motor vehicles, fuels, electrical machinery, heavy industrial machinery, food
Imports – Main Partners	United States, 19%; Argentina, 16%; Brazil, 7%; China, 6%; Japan, 4% (2000)

History at a Glance

1541	Pedro de Valdivia arrives in the Central Valley and founds Santiago.
1553	Pedro de Valdivia, now the first governor of Chile, is killed at the hands of the Mapuche Indians.
1810	Chile declares independence on September 18.
1810–1818	Chile's War of Independence.
1818–1823	Bernardo O'Higgins serves as Chile's first president.
1823	Slavery is abolished.
1830–1837	Diego Portales dominates politics.
1833	Diego Portales oversees a new constitution based on a strong presidential government. The constitution lasts until 1891.
1836–1839	Chile fights a war against the Peruvian-Bolivian Confederation.
1840	William Wheelwright, an American industrialist, creates the first steamship line.
1851	William Wheelwright builds Chile's first railroad.
1860	Chile becomes the world's leading copper exporter.
1879–1884	The War of the Pacific takes place. Chile is pitted against its former rivals, Peru and Bolivia. Chile is the victor.
1891	Civil War erupts in Chile, pitting the executive branch, under President José Manuel Balmaceda, against Congress. Balmaceda manages to end his term and commits suicide. Technically, his government is not overthrown.
1891	A new constitution establishes a parliamentary form of government. The constitution lasts until 1925, when the parliamentary system is abolished.
1907	Government troops massacre nitrate workers at Santa María de Iquique. This begins the movement to unionize miners and lays the groundwork for the Communist Party movement a decade later.
1925	The government amends its constitution. The changes gives the government the job of providing social security; setting standards for public health, housing, and sanitation; and enforcing safety regulations in the workplace.
1928–1931	Colonel Carlos Ibáñez leads a military coup and assumes dictatorial powers.
1934	Women gain the right to vote in municipal elections.
1949	Women gain the right to vote in national elections.

1952–1958	Carlos Ibáñez, the former dictator, returns to power. This time he is elected.
1958–1964	Jorge Alessandri, the son of a former president, serves as president.
1964–1970	Eduardo Frei-Montalva is President.
1970–1973	Salvador Allende, a Marxist, is elected President. He is the first Marxist to be elected president in a democracy.
1973	A military coup overthrows Allende.
1973–1990	General Augusto Pinochet leads the government. Officially he leads a constitutional government. In fact, he is a dictator who leads a brutally repressive regime.
1978	Chile and Bolivia break off diplomatic relations due to a dispute over establishing a land corridor to the Pacific for Bolivia.
1981	The Constitution of 1981 is passed. Revisions in 1989, 1993 and 1997 will transform the constitution into a democratic document.
1990	Pinochet ends his rule, because of his loss in a 1989 plebiscite calling for the people to vote "yes" or "no" on whether they wanted him in office.
1990–1994	Patricio Aylwin serves a single four-year term as President.
1990	President Aylwin creates the National Truth and Reconciliation Commission to investigate atrocities of the Pinochet regime.
1996	Chile signs a Free Trade Agreement with Canada.
1998	Chile hosts the second Summit of the Americas in 1998 and signs a Free Trade Agreement with Mexico.
1994–2000	Eduardo Frei Fuiz-Tagle, son of a former Chilean president, serves a six-year term as President.
2000	Ricardo Lagos is elected to six-year term as President.
2001	Chile presides over of the Rio Group (an organization of 19 Latin American and Caribbean countries) in 2001.
2002	Chile signs a Free Trade Agreements with Costa Rica and El Salvador.
2003	Chile signs a Free Trade Agreements with the United States, European Union, South Korea, and European Free Trade Association (Iceland, Liechtenstein, Norway, and Switzerland). Pinochet is placed under house arrest, but the Santiago appeals court closes the case, declaring the former dictator unfit for trial for health reasons.

Glossary

Aísen: Chile's eleventh administrative division (also Region XI).

Andes: The largest major mountain system in South America.

Andean condor: The national bird of Chile.

Antofagasta: Chile's second administrative division (also Region II). Its namesake is the city of Antofagasta, the largest city of the division.

Altiplano: In Spanish, "high plain." This is an elevated Andean plain that stretches across the borders separating Argentina, Bolivia, Chile, and Peru.

Araucania: Chile's ninth administrative division (also Region IX). It is the homeland of the Araucanian Indians (see below).

Araucanian: The general name applied to the Indians occupying the valleys just south of the Bío Bío River at the time of European arrival.

Atacama: Chile's third administrative division (also Region III).

Aymara: The main indigenous Indian group in the Andes altiplano region of Bolivia, Argentina, Peru, and Chile.

Bío Bío: Chile's seventh administrative division (also Region VII). Its namesake is the Bío Bío River. Concepción is the largest city in the division.

Callampa: Chilean word for mushroom and slang for shantytown, a hastily built settlement on the edge of a city.

Communism: A one-party political system that leads a nation toward Marxist socialism.

Conservative: In politics, a person or party that wishes to preserve traditions or existing governmental institutions and opposes any changes to these.

Coquimbo: Chile's fourth administrative division (also Region IV). Its namesake is the city of Coquimbo, the largest city in the division.

Criollo: In Chile, a *criollo* is a Spaniard born in America.

Cuenca: The national dance of Chile.

Encomienda **system:** The Spanish colonial system that allowed an individual Spaniard to use Indians for labor in a particular area.

FTA: See Free Trade Agreement.

Free Trade Agreement (FTA): This agreement charges no taxes or very low taxes on goods that countries exchange, in order to reduce the prices of the goods.

Garúa: A thick summer fog that forms over the cold Humboldt Current.

Gaucho: Argentine cowboys, who became legendary in song, prose, and poetry. Gauchos migrated into Chile's Patagonia areas, east of the Andes.

Huemul: This large deer appears on Chile's coat of arms, but Chileans hunted it to near extinction.

Humboldt Current: A north-flowing ocean current that affects Chile's climate and agriculture.

Inquilino: A tenant farmer who works for an estate owner for little or no pay. In return, the *inquilino* lives on the estate with his family and farms a small plot of land.

Liberal: In politics, a person or party that favors governmental change or reforms to institutions that gives freedom that is more personal to the individual.

Los Lagos: The Lakes in Spanish. This is the name of Chile's tenth administrative division (also Region X).

Magallanes: Chile's twelfth administrative division (also Region XII). This is the southernmost region of Chile and includes Tierra del Fuego.

Mapuche: The warlike Araucanian tribe that survived the Spanish invasion and fought the Spaniards until the 1880s; it is the most populous native group in Chile today.

Maule: Chile's seventh administrative division (also Region VII).

Mestizo: People of mixed Indian and European ancestry. Mestizos make up about 70% of Chile's population.

Marxist-Leninist socialism: The belief that society should be classless, the state should own all means of production, and all workers should perform equal work and receive equal pay. (See Communism).

Metropolitan Santiago: The smallest but most populous of Chile's 13 administrative divisions.

Mercosur: Spanish acronym for Southern Cone Common Market. Argentina, Brazil, Paraguay and Uruguay are the main members. Chile is an associate member.

Glossary

Mount Aconcagua: Highest peak in the Andes Mountains and the Southern Hemisphere. It is located in Argentina near the Argentine-Chilean boundary.

New Song: A type of Chilean folk music inspired by the hardships of poor miners, tenant farmers, and factory workers.

O'Higgins, General Bernardo: The Chilean nation's George Washington. He is the namesake of Chile's sixth administrative division (also Region VI).

Patagonia: A Texas-size desert plateau region that makes up most of southern Argentina; small areas extend into Chile.

Panaderia: A small neighborhood bakery.

Peninsulares: The *peninsulares* were colonial Spaniards born in the country of Spain, which is part of the Iberian Peninsula.

Pudú: The world's smallest deer; Chileans have hunted it to near extinction.

Rainshadow: A dry area behind rain-blocking mountains.

Tarapacá: Chile's first administrative division (also Region I). The namesake of this region is the largest town in this desert region.

Valparaíso: Chile's fifth administrative division (also Region V). The namesake of this region is the coastal city of the same name.

Viceroyalty: The largest administrative division in the Spanish Empire.

Allende, Isabel. *My Invented Country: A Nostalgic Journey Through Chile.* Translated from the Spanish by Margaret Sayers. New York: HarperCollins Publishers, 2003.

Bowman, Isaiah. *Desert Trails of Atacama.* New York: America Geographical Society, 1924.

Castillo-Feliú, David William, Melissa Fitch Lockhart, and Darrell B. Lockhart. *Culture and Customs of Chile.* Westport, CN: Greenwood Press, 2000.

Central Intelligence Agency. *CIA Fact Book.* Washington, D.C.: U.S. Government Printing Office, 2002.

Ercilla y Zúñiga, Alonso de. *La Araucana.* Madrid: Ediciones Catedra, 2000.

Minnis, Natalie. *Insight Guide: Chile.* Maspeth, NY: Langenscheidt Publishers, Inc., 2000.

Mistral, Gabriela. *The Selected Poems of Gabriela Mistral.* Translated from the Spanish by Langston Hughes. Bloomington: Indiana University Press, 1957.

Neruda, Pablo, *Selected Poems.* Translated by Nathaniel Tarn. Boston: Houghton Mifflin, [1970], 1990.

Toledo Olivares, Ximena, and Eduardo Zapater Alvarado. *Geographía General y Regional de Chile.* Santiago, Chile: Editorial Universitaria, 1991.

WEBSITES

Chile. Nationmaster.com.
  http://www.nationmaster.com.

Condorito. Yahoo, Inc.
  http://espanol.entertainment.yahoo.com/comics/condorita.

Pablo Neruda. Blues for Peace.
  http://www.bluesforpeace.com/neruda.htm.

Victor Jara. Lyrics Connection.
  http://www.arlo.net/lyrics/victor-jara.shtml.

Index

Index

Index

Index

Index

page:

9:      © Lucidity Information Design, LLC
13:     © Lucidity Information Design, LLC
15:     New Millennium Images
20:     New Millennium Images
28:     © Grahm Deden; Ecoscene/CORBIS
34:     AFP/NMI
40:     © CORBIS
48:     AFP/NMI
55:     KRT/NMI
59:     AP/Wide World Photos
63:     © Peter Guttman/CORBIS

69:     Notimex/NMI
71:     AFP/NMI
77:     21st Century Publishing
84:     KRT/NMI
87:     Notimex/NMI
97:     Reuters Photo Archive/NMI
105:    Reuters Photo Archive/NMI
107:    KRT/NMI
114:    AP/Wide World Photos
118:    AP/Wide World Photos

Cover: New Millennium Images

About the Author

DR. RICHARD A. CROOKER is a geography professor at Kutztown University in Pennsylvania, where he teaches physical geography, oceanography, map reading, and climatology. He received a Ph.D. in Geography from the University of California, Riverside. Dr. Crooker is a member of the Association of American Geographers and the National Council for Geographic Education. He has received numerous research grants, including three from the National Geographical Society. His publications deal with a wide range of geographical topics. He enjoys reading, hiking, bicycling, kayaking and boogie boarding.

CHARLES F. ("FRITZ") GRITZNER is Distinguished Professor of Geography at South Dakota University in Brookings. He is now in his fifth decade of college teaching and research. During his career, he has taught more than 60 different courses, spanning the fields of physical, cultural, and regional geography. In addition to his teaching, he enjoys writing, working with teachers, and sharing his love for geography with students. As consulting editor for the MODERN WORLD NATIONS series, he has a wonderful opportunity to combine each of these "hobbies." Fritz has served as both President and Executive Director of the National Council for Geographic Education and has received the Council's highest honor, the George J. Miller Award for Distinguished Service.